The Films of
LAUREL & HARDY

By the same author

The Films of
LAUREL & HARDY

by WILLIAM K. EVERSON

THE CITADEL PRESS *SECAUCUS, NEW JERSEY*

ACKNOWLEDGMENTS

Grateful acknowledgment is made to the following individuals and institutions for their help in filling in some of the gaps in my still files by contributing rare photographs from their own collections:

John E. Allen
Kevin Brownlow
James Card (George Eastman House)
Carlos Clarens
Herbert Gelbspan (Hal Roach Studios)
Gerald D. McDonald
Charles Turner
Robert G. Youngson
The British Film Institute
Entertainment Films

Published by Citadel Press
A division of Lyle Stuart Inc.
120 Enterprise Ave., Secaucus, N.J. 07094
In Canada: Musson Book Company
A division of General Publishing Co. Limited
Manufactured in the United States of America
ISBN 0-8065-0146-4

Contents

Stan Laurel	9
Oliver Hardy	11
Introduction	15
The Years Before the Teaming	19
The Modus Operandi of Laurel & Hardy	27
The Films of Laurel & Hardy	39
Forty-Five Minutes from Hollywood	41
Duck Soup	41
Slipping Wives	41
Love 'Em and Weep	42
Why Girls Love Sailors	43
With Love and Hisses	44
Sailors Beware	44
Do Detectives Think?	45
Flying Elephants	47
Sugar Daddies	48
Call of the Cuckoo	49
The Second Hundred Years	50
Hats Off	52
Putting Pants on Philip	53
The Battle of the Century	55
Leave 'Em Laughing	56
The Finishing Touch	58
From Soup to Nuts	60

You're Darn Tootin'	62
Their Purple Moment	64
Should Married Men Go Home?	65
Early to Bed	67
Two Tars	68
Habeas Corpus	71
We Faw Down	72
Liberty	73
Wrong Again	76
That's My Wife	77
Big Business	78
Double Whoopee	80
Berth Marks	83
Men O' War	85
A Perfect Day	87
They Go Boom	88
Bacon Grabbers	90
Angora Love	90
Unaccustomed as We Are	91
Hollywood Review of 1929	92
Hoosegow	93
Night Owls	94
Blotto	96
Rogue Song	97
Be Big	98

Brats	99	Going Bye Bye	157
Below Zero	101	Them Thar Hills	158
The Laurel & Hardy Murder Case	102	Babes in Toyland	160
Hog Wild	103	The Live Ghost	163
Another Fine Mess	106	Tit for Tat	165
Chickens Come Home	107	The Fixer-Uppers	167
Laughing Gravy	108	Thicker Than Water	168
Our Wife	109	Bonnie Scotland	169
Come Clean	110	The Bohemian Girl	171
Pardon Us	113	Our Relations	173
One Good Turn	116	Way Out West	176
Beau Hunks	118	Pick a Star	181
Helpmates	120	Swiss Miss	182
Any Old Port	122	Blockheads	185
The Music Box	123	1939	189
The Chimp	125	The Flying Deuces	190
County Hospital	128	A Chump at Oxford	192
Scram	129	Saps at Sea	194
Pack Up Your Troubles	131	1941	196
Their First Mistake	132	Great Guns	198
Towed in a Hole	135	A-Haunting We Will Go	199
Twice Two	137	Air Raid Wardens	200
Me and My Pal	139	Jitterbugs	201
Fra Diavolo	140	The Dancing Masters	202
The Midnight Patrol	143	The Big Noise	204
Busy Bodies	145	Nothing But Trouble	207
Dirty Work	148	The Bullfighters	208
Sons of the Desert	151	Atoll K	209
The Private Life of Oliver the Eighth	155	The Compilations	212
Hollywood Party	156	Deleted Scenes	216

Stan Laurel

June 16, 1895 – February 23, 1965

Born Arthur Stanley Jefferson in Ulverston, Lancashire, England, Laurel came of a theatrical family. His father had been a prominent theatrical impresario—embracing writing, acting, and managing theatres—in the late 1800's, and from childhood Stanley had nursed a burning zeal to go on the stage too. His key ambition was to achieve success as a comic in the music halls, and as soon as he was finished with his cursory education (acquired largely, and reluctantly, at the King James Grammar School in Bishop Auckland), he made his stage debut at Pickard's Museum, a small Glasgow theatre. He was just sixteen. Lupino Lane, slightly ahead of Laurel in his rise to fame, was one of his contemporaries on the boards at this time, and Lane too—though his greatest fame would be on the London stage—would become a popular Hollywood comedian of the 20's. Eventually Laurel joined Fred Karno's famed theatrical troupe, and after two or three years, the troupe came to America. This was in 1910. Karno's best-loved routine was "Mumming Birds," or "A Night in an English Music Hall," as it was retitled in the United

States. In time, the sketch came to be a showcase for Charlie Chaplin, and Laurel understudied him, occasionally getting a chance to perform the act himself. When Chaplin left Karno in 1913 to accept a more lucrative offer from Mack Sennett and the movies, the Karno troupe foundered, so essential had Chaplin become to its box-office value. By now, however, Laurel was an accomplished pantomimist, and he had no trouble working up other comedy acts and touring the American vaudeville houses. It was during this period that he changed his show business name to Stan Laurel, and it was while performing in a comedy routine in 1917 that he was noticed by a small independent producer and invited to make a film. A comedy two-reeler, *Nuts in May,* was the result, and it was funny enough to convince Laurel that his future lay in film. Nominal stardom came fairly rapidly, though front-rank stardom was still almost a decade away, awaiting his fortuitous teaming with Oliver Hardy.

Although he was beset by a series of illnesses and strokes, Laurel's final years were happy ones. His mind remained active, alert, and cognizant of the comedy in everyday life until the very end. He was gratified by the belated recognition of the value of his work, was given an honorary Academy Award, and spent much time discussing comedy style—or writing long letters to his friends. One of his last acts was to work with Jack McCabe, author of *Mr. Laurel and Mr. Hardy,* in setting up a delightful group known as The Sons of the Desert. Organized somewhat on the lines of the Variety Clubs, with "tents" in different cities (all of them named after Laurel & Hardy films—e.g., the "Another Fine Mess" tent), its aims included the preservation of film, the setting up of a Stan Laurel scholarship, but most of all the sheer enjoyment of frequent gatherings to screen Laurel & Hardy films. Stan himself constructed the deliberately nonsensical "constitution," which in itself lampooned the serious mumbo-jumbo of the original Sons of the Desert group (in their 1934 film of that name), and made sure that the group would be neither an academic one, nor an adulatory fan club. Laurel's widow and comedian Raymond Walburn were among the guests at early meetings, and the group, among other things, has uncovered a great deal of newsreel and home movie footage of Laurel with his father, and of Laurel & Hardy on tour, to tumultuous receptions, in England in the 30's. Thus far the number one unrealized project has been the rediscovery of an odd little film that Laurel & Hardy appeared in for the Masquers Club in the early 30's, doing a fragmentary sketch with a balky automobile.

Oliver Hardy

January 18, 1892 – August 7, 1957

Hardy, whose full name, Oliver Norvelle Hardy, was the one that he used in his films, since he liked the dignified sound of it, was born in Harlem, Georgia. His parents were of English and Scottish descent, and unlike Laurel's forebears, presented not a trace of show business ancestry or ambition. Communal singing was a family hobby, however, and probably because of this Hardy took singing lessons, and took them so seriously that for a while, and at the tender age of eight, he was performing professionally with a minstrel show. While this career didn't last (not because of any shortcomings on Hardy's part, but because he wasn't as yet dedicated to a show business career), it did convince him that a continuance of his singing studies would be worthwhile. Although his subsequent comedy career didn't exactly exploit his musical ta!ent, his rich voice was occasionally put to good use, particularly in the straightforward and charming rendering of the same kind of Southern ballads that he had sung as a child minstrel.

A tentative stab at studying law was abandoned when Hardy got his first real taste of the movie business by opening a small theatre in 1910. Movies intrigued Hardy from the beginning, and since it was much easier to break into films in those days (especially as it wasn't being done by respectable people!), he decided to have a try at comedy acting—something that his already quite substantial size suggested he'd be most suited to. He joined the Lubin Company in Florida in 1913. His first film of note, *The Paperhanger's Helper,* came in 1915. Coincidentally (?) quite similar to Chaplin's *Work,* likewise a 1915 release, it was in itself a primitive blueprint for the later Laurel & Hardy comedies, both in its comedy teamwork (Bobby Ray was his partner) and in its comedy content. From here Hardy moved on to the Billy West, Larry Semon, and other comedies which are discussed more fully elsewhere in this book.

Hardy, like Laurel, was plagued with illness in the last years of his life, and lost a great deal of weight. Also like Laurel, however, while his ambulatory powers were reduced, he lost neither his sense of humor nor his zest for living, and within the irksome limits of reduced activity, his final years were also peaceful and contented ones.

Introduction

Introduction

It has suddenly become the "in" thing to be Laurel & Hardy admirers. The spectacular, but labored and only intermittently funny, comedy "special" *The Great Race* (1965) was "dedicated" to Laurel & Hardy, which was a nice and doubtless sincerely meant tribute, although it's a pity that it couldn't have been a film more worthy of them. The controversial and not wholly successful *The Loved One,* also from 1965, actually had far more kinship with some aspects of their comedy, and I suspect that, given a choice, they would have preferred their dedication on *that* film.

The cult worship that so often follows the belated discovery, or rediscovery, of unrecognized stars (or for that matter directors or writers) can be a both annoying and dangerous thing. Annoying because most of the analyses and tributes *were* made earlier, albeit in less pretentious terms. Dangerous because over-adulation can often build up a wall of resent-ment against its objects, who are usually wholly innocent of any involvement in or promotion of a cult-movement, often dislike it, and usually refuse to take it seriously. There's danger too in that the object of sudden hero-worship *may* begin to take his disciples too seriously and try to live up to the interpretations they have imposed on his work. For a while, in the 20's, this happened to Charlie Chaplin. More recently, William Wyler, Alfred Hitchcock, Robert Wise, Joseph Losey and George Stevens are just a few of the fine film craftsmen who put their best and most cinematic work behind them when their cults insisted (perhaps rightly, but at the wrong time) that they were artists and geniuses of the first magnitude. What a pity it is that most cultists are sheep, unwilling to express their enthusiasm until it is fashionable to do so and until time has proven them right beyond any possibility of contradiction. If the cults have any value at all, it would be when the targets of their bouquets are still young, fresh, and experimental. Then the prestige of cult-support might warrant really important properties being tossed their way when they are creatively best equipped to handle them.

Now Laurel & Hardy are a cult. It's a trifle grating (not that they don't warrant the widest acclaim and a position on the same pedestal with Keaton and Chaplin) and the immediate reaction to all of the Johnny-come-lately critics is, "Fine, but where were you when the boys were *making* all of these films that you now analyze in such minute detail?" The answer, of course, is that they were either too young (hardly their fault, although it doesn't excuse the rather egocentric attitude that their generation is the first really to appreciate Laurel & Hardy), or that they were too busy building other and then more fashionable cults—to Lubitsch, perhaps, or to the Marx Brothers.

Fortunately, Laurel & Hardy will survive all this. So many of the "best" cults are based on general unavailability of the films, thus having a snob value as well. It's easy to foster a Louise Brooks cult (no slight intended, for the lady is a good friend of mine, a perceptive film critic, and certainly one of the most magnetic of all movie personalities) when her films can only be seen by those fortunate enough to have entry to the archives, and when the written words and hymns of praise cannot be disputed. The Laurel & Hardy films are around more than ever—in their original form, in the fine compilations constructed by Robert Youngson, on television, in theatres, even in 16mm and 8mm home movie form for the permanent delight of both student and plain admirer. Furthermore, almost all of their films have been preserved,

only three or four of the earlier ones apparently having vanished, and even these may well turn up eventually. Too, the cult-worship comes too late to affect their wonderful performing style and unique film grammar; at worst it can only send the imitation Laurel & Hardy merchants off on the wrong track, a fate they richly deserve.

Cults don't last too long. Bergman and Godard have already "had it." Antonioni and Resnais should get the axe next. Maybe in a year or two the Laurel & Hardy cult will die too, perhaps when the Wheeler and Woolsey or Jack Benny movies of the 30's become the new "in" thing. Then all that will be left will be those of us who love their work, and have always loved it. And of course, the Laurel & Hardy films, where even the flaws and weaknesses are somehow part of a consistent pattern.

I don't think any comedians have ever brought more laughter to the world than Laurel & Hardy. Keaton was wittier and cleverer, Chaplin a greater overall artist and dramatist. But in terms of sheer laugh content and brilliance of comic invention and construction, Laurel & Hardy take second place to no one. Their humor is universal and timeless, and inevitably—owing to the dearth of original comedy creators in the field today—their comedies must seem even funnier as time goes on. So I suppose it's useless to complain about the Laurel & Hardy "cult." There's bound to be another one in 2036, with perhaps a special one-hundredth anniversary screening of *Our Relations;* and another renaissance a few hundred years later. And who knows what the prints will be like by then? (Some of them aren't so good even now!) Let's just enjoy them while we can.

The Years Before the Teaming

An early publicity shot of
Stan Laurel.

The Years Before the Teaming

Next to Chaplin's, no faces are more familiar to lovers of screen comedy than those of Laurel & Hardy—although many people never sorted out which was which, and continued to identify them only as "the fat one" and "the thin one." Perhaps it was something of a tribute to the complete fusing of their so-different personalities into one perfect team that it never seemed to matter which was which. Because it was to him that the *precipitation* of most of the comedy fell and because his was more the traditional clown face, it is Stan Laurel who is often considered the funnier of the two. However, discussion on this is pointless; Laurel was a pure clown, Hardy a subtler pantomimist and even something of an actor. Laurel had a long, simple-looking face with a wide mouth that could spread into an elongated clownish grin, or pucker up into childish grimaces. The eyes could reflect dull-witted, uncomprehending stupidity, or they could fill with tears at a moment's notice. The tall forehead, furrowed with lines of perplexity, was topped by a scruffy tuft of uncombed hair that was frequently scratched in a futile effort to solve some weighty problem. Conversely, Oliver Hardy's face—kindly, cherubic, a fringe of hair across the top of his forehead (suggesting that his barber used a bowl to guide his scissors), double chins to the south, and a dapper but rather pointless moustache in between—was not that of a clown, nor was it funny in itself. It was what Hardy did with that face—the mute appeals to the audience, the combination of pain, indignity, and resignation in those expressive eyes—that made it funny. Together they made the finest comedy team in the business, and unlike most teams, neither was a stooge for the other, nor one a "straight man" to keep plot and romantic complications moving along. Both were admirable comedians and pantomimists in their own right, and when talkies came in, their voices matched their visual personalities so perfectly that they went on to even greater success. Apart from being a brilliant comic in front of the camera, Laurel was also brilliant behind the camera. It was he who devised many of their funniest routines, and at times he also functioned as producer or director.

However, apart from the accident of being cast together in an independent comedy of 1917 titled *Lucky Dog,* Laurel & Hardy didn't come together as a team until as late as 1926. Before that, both had had long careers on their own in silent comedies.

Laurel had been far more successful as a solo comedian, perhaps because he *looked* more like a clown than Hardy did—and being slimmer, fitted more logically into the boy-chases-girl situations that formed the continuities of so many one- and two-reelers. Also, as a writer and director he learned more about the construction of comedy, and thus knew how to build his own screen character. That character was vastly different from the one that finally emerged from the Laurel-Hardy combination. The early Stan Laurel was rarely a simple-minded goof. His costume suggested something of the clown; he wore normal clothes, but they were usually a size

19

or two too big, and this he often emphasized by wearing a collar *so* big that it more resembled a horse collar. This kind of costume established him, literally, as a misfit—but he usually wore a straw hat too, which told audiences that though he was a misfit, he was a dapper and worldly-wise one. The crying routine that later became so famous in his films opposite Hardy was rarely in evidence; if something went wrong with the plans of this early Stan Laurel, he wasted no time crying about it, but took decisive (and sometimes savagely vindictive) action to remedy it. And he never seemed to scratch that unruly mop of his. For one thing, it was neatly combed and kept in place with Vaseline. For another, this Laurel was a cunning fellow; if he was puzzled or confused, he'd never tip his hand by showing it so openly. In fact, he was something of a sharpie, and not too far removed from the character that W. C. Fields was to create. Laurel, however, wasn't quite so delightfully despicable as Fields. Fields was usually lazy, and diligent at sidestepping honest work. Laurel, to the contrary, was a very hard worker: a high-pressure salesman in *Kill or Cure,* or an energetic fruit-packer in *Oranges and Lemons.* But if he found that hard work wasn't enough, he wasn't above a good deal of chiselling or exploiting of his fellow-workers to get what he wanted. And when thwarted, he was vengeful in the extreme. The later Laurel was too, but only in the way that a small boy hits back in anger and frustration. The early Laurel just couldn't bear the thought of anyone getting the better of him, and would be quite merciless in dealing with anyone who, deliberately or otherwise, found himself in that position. The early Laurel seems to have inherited a

great deal of the thoughtlessness and casual sadism in dealing with others—"enemies" and innocent by-standers alike—that marked the first, violent, Charlie Chaplin comedies. *Kill or Cure,* for example, opens with patent-medicine salesman Laurel giving an eloquent and breathless pep talk to a prospective customer, who is leaning languidly and disinterestedly against a gate. Finally, when Laurel pauses for breath, a bespectacled gentleman, clearly a doctor, enters the scene and addresses the customer in sign language. They both move away, to reveal that the unresponsive customer had been standing in front of a sign identifying his "home" as a deaf and dumb institute. From inside the grounds comes a woman, another prospective client. Half hoping for a sale, half getting even for his wasted time, he berates her with an exaggerated and insulting pantomime of sign language. Of course, she is *not* an inmate, but a voluble and aggressive woman who promptly vents her spleen on him. Another typical gag from a solo Laurel comedy of this early-20's period: In *Man About Town,* store-detective James Finlayson spots a woman shoplifter pilfering items and secreting them in her suspiciously bulging coat. Accosting her, Finlayson shakes his captive, and the tell-tale purloined goods fall to the floor from beneath her coat. With a satisfied smirk, Finlayson moves on, and at the next counter spots another obvious shoplifter. It is a wizened little old man, who would seem to have stuffed stolen merchandise down the back of his jacket. With his customary little jig of triumph, Finlayson pounces on his victim and pushes his jacket up. The man of course is a genuine hunchback! If such gags seem tasteless or "sick," it should be re-

20

Oliver Hardy's dignity dampened well before his association with Stan.

membered that comedy in the silent era was a wide-open field. Race, religion, minority groups, sex, all of these things were kidded mercilessly, and because they were kidded equally, there was never any feeling of discrimination or resentment, as long as the individual gags were funny—as they usually were. However, this comedy of cruelty (and pain and embarrassment *can* be very funny) obviously became ingrained in Laurel's work at this time, for one finds this kind of gag used constantly, and effectively, in the later Laurel & Hardy films, long after they had been discarded by almost all other comics.

In the very early twenties, Stan Laurel made a series of comedies for Metro release, under the production supervision of G. M. Anderson, the former "Broncho Billy." Most of these comedies, devised by Laurel himself, were clever but extremely variable satires of current boxoffice hits. Some of them were funny only if one knew well the films they were spoofing; *Under Two Jags,* for example, a takeoff on the Priscilla Dean Foreign Legion adventure, *Under Two Flags,* meticulously reconstructs situations and costumes, and is amusing when directly juxtaposed with its inspiration, but on its own it is singularly unfunny. *Mud and Sand,* a satire of Valentino's *Blood and Sand,* is too protracted and labored, but its best gags comment beautifully on some of the absurdities of the original. Conversely, some of Laurel's spoofs in this series hold up superbly well as separate entities: *The Soilers* (kidding that rugged Rex Beach adventure *The Spoilers)* is an appropriate satire of an entire genre. Its oversized saloon battle is a slapstick gem, and the injection of a fey homosexual into such a

thoroughly masculine environment provided both surprise and comic shock values. But Anderson and Laurel had trouble dealing with Metro head Louis B. Mayer—an old story for many directors and stars—and the series dissolved. Anderson went into retirement, and Laurel joined Hal Roach, a move that was to further establish him as a popular comic, and pave the way for the ultimate teaming with Oliver Hardy.

Between 1923 and 1926, Laurel made a great

many one- and two-reel solo comedies on the Hal Roach lot. Some, like *Should Tall Men Marry?,* were frankly unfunny and a sheer waste of his talent. But comedians in those days had to turn out so many comedies to a rigid schedule that a few duds were unavoidable. On the whole, both Roach's and Laurel's standards remained remarkably high, and films like the already-mentioned *Oranges and Lemons, Kill or Cure* and *Man About Town* offered an impressive array of Laurel comedy, ranging from the satiric to the plain slapstick. But whatever the circumstances of plot, the Laurel character remained essentially the same—aggressive, brash, resourceful, not particularly lovable, but certainly amusing. There's no time spent on sentiment or pathos: while Stan may be a playboy trying to flirt with a girl, he has no thought of winning or wooing her seriously, or of proving his ability. His only concern is to come out on top. These comparatively unfamiliar comedies would doubtless prove an eye-opener to contemporary audiences who associate Laurel only with the "Stan and Ollie" team. They show what a funny man Stan could be on his own, but they also show why he could never have become really great had he stuck to this screen character. As an "unsympathetic" comic, he lacked the depth and the flawlessly refined anti-social qualities of W. C. Fields. He was merely a fresh guy who wasn't outrageous enough to be continually shocking. And at the same time, he was an enterprising and likeable-looking fellow without any really admirable qualities. He was caught very much between two schools of comedy. Doubtless Laurel realized it himself, which is probably why he continued to ply his trade as a director. But if his unique talent was being improperly channelled, it was still a talent that was too real to be held in check for long.

Oliver Hardy, now also a fixture on the Hal Roach lot, was being wasted and misused in an even more lamentable fashion. His career in movies pre-dated Laurel's by quite a few years, since he started with the Lubin Company in 1913, but he never achieved any kind of status as a solo comedian. He soon became to comics Billy West and Larry Semon what Eric Campbell had been to Chaplin—the stock comic villain. Indeed, since West was the foremost Chaplin imitator, and so adept and convincing at his masquerade that many of his comedies are accepted by the uninitiated as the real thing, it is highly probable that Hardy's burlesque villainy in the West comedies of 1918 was intended as a deliberate imitation of Campbell. In both the West films and the later Larry

Semon two-reelers for Vitagraph, Hardy's perennial character was as the burlesqued Victorian stage heavy: elegantly dressed, top-hatted, mustachio-twirling, and often in pursuit of the heroine's virtue as energetically as he chased ill-gotten gains. Hardy's bulk enabled him to play a convincing roughneck at times, too. With torn and dirty shirt, unshaven jowls, black eye make-up, generously applied scars and a sinister eye-patch, he made a fearsome-looking villainous seaman in, for example, Semon's *The Boy Friend.* But his villainy paid off best when he was attired in sartorial elegance, such trappings giving freer rein to Hardy's inspired pantomimings of mock elegance, thwarted rage, and blustering pomposity. Too, West's and Semon's villains had to take a lot of punishment, such as being hit with buckets of goo or dumped into mud puddles, and the necessary comic contrast of messy indignity descending upon and deflating a figure of bombast made Hardy's dapper and polished exterior a must. For a man of his size, Hardy was astonishingly agile, and entered into all the mayhem with spirit, rarely resorting to a double. Semon obviously appreciated him, for he used him prominently in all of his shorts, as well as in his feature *The Wizard of Oz.* However, equally obviously, Semon was aware of Hardy's scene-stealing propensities, for while the Semon comedies are full of close-ups of Larry Semon mugging and reacting, Hardy's villainy was perpetrated almost entirely in long and medium shots!

Hardy has never been considered a "creative" comedian in the sense of working out plots and gags in advance, though he certainly contributed important story ideas and bits of business while shooting was in progress. Laurel later recalled, affectionately, that once Hardy had finished before the cameras, he liked to be lazy, or enjoy himself at golf, but had little interest in participating in script conferences. Be this as it may, he would appear to have had a retentive and imaginative memory, for some of the brightest gags in the later Laurel & Hardy films can be seen to have had their roots in these earlier comedies with Hardy as the heavy. Their brilliant early talkie *Brats* would seem to have sprung from a pre-1920 Billy West comedy *Playmates,* in which Hardy and West appear as petulant children.

Hardy's other early 20's work included an appearance in Buster Keaton's *The Three Ages,* and some villain and character work in Buck Jones westerns. It was another western, 1924's *Rex, King of the Wild Horses,* that finally established him at the

Stan Laurel with Lillian Rich in one of his solo starring comedies for Hal Roach, *On the Front Page*.

Hal Roach studios. For two or three years, it must be admitted, Roach had no idea what to do with him. He was merely a contract player used in two-reel comedies, and with far less prominence than he had been enjoying in the Billy West or Larry Semon films. But the image of Victorian villainy was allowed to lapse; Hardy's roles were minor, but they permitted him to be seen without makeup and to do little vignettes in which he could try out and polish the comedy "business" that would soon be rounded out and integrated into a finished comic character. In these comedies with Charlie Chase, Mabel Normand, and others, we find Hardy introducing the direct stare at the audience, the bullish run, the smile of coy embarrassment—like a naughty child caught doing something wrong—that slowly spreads over his whole cherubic face, accompanied by squirming feet and twisting hands; the florid gestures with his hands; and a whole range of subtle facial expressions. There's a marvelous moment in Charlie Chase's *Fluttering Hearts* in which Charlie seeks to lure Hardy to a darkened corner of a speakeasy and uses a seductive-looking store dummy to achieve that end. Hidden behind a curtain, Chase's hands manipulate the dummy and give it life, even to raising its skirt slightly above the knee in the traditional come-hither manner. But at one point he miscalculates, and what was intended as a tantalizing exposure of knee becomes an obscenely outrageous display of the entire thigh. Flirtatious Hardy, watching, manages with a quick gulp and wide-opened eyes to express shock, embarrassment, and lecherous expectation all within the space of a one-second closeup! In Mabel Normand's *The Nickelhopper,* he was a joyously unrestrained jazz drummer in a sleazy dance-hall sequence that also featured a likewise unbilled Boris Karloff; in Charlie Chase's *Crazy Like a Fox* he pantomimed reaction to a display of insanity by Charlie, and in another Chase comedy, *Long Fliv the King,* he was a uniformed Ruritanian general whose aplomb and resplendent uniform are both ruined by a scoop of ice cream. In all of these films Hardy was called upon to react to a given situation rather than to create it, and by and large this came to be the formula that would evolve when, in 1926, he finally came to be teamed with Stan Laurel. Perhaps "team" is too grandiose a term to apply to their early films. They appeared *together,* and while in their first films

23

they seemed, naturally, to gravitate together as a team, their comedy material was not constructed with teamwork in mind. In retrospect, it is even a little surprising that it took producer Hal Roach so long, after their initial films together, to recognize their enormous potential as a team. But there hadn't been a major comedy team on the screen since the days of Keaton and Arbuckle. All the big comics worked solo. The minor teams that Sennett developed—Harry Langdon and Vernon Dent, Billy Bevan and Andy Clyde—were not *consistently* teamed, and in any case fell into the standard pattern of a first comic supported by a stooge. Certainly Roach had no way of knowing that in Laurel & Hardy he had a combination that would not only turn out to be the most popular screen comedy team of all time, but would also inspire perpetual repetition through the years, from Abbott & Costello and Martin & Lewis on probably into infinity. Despite being a little slow on the uptake in recognizing his new stars' worth, Roach deserves credit for giving them a completely free hand to develop their own style when he did recognize it, and therein perhaps lies the secret of a comedy career that was far more successful than Mack Sennett's. Sennett established a formula, and never deviated from it. As the years went by, his films became slicker, funnier, faster, but the basic pattern of sight gag and chase never changed. He discovered and nurtured top comedians like Chaplin and Langdon and then lost them because, quite rightly, they wanted to progress from knockabout to subtler forms of comedy. From the beginning, with his first Harold Lloyd films, Roach had aimed at adding sophistication and "prestige" to his films. Sometimes he failed. He was wrong, for example, in thinking that big name stars would automatically enhance the value of short comedies. Obviously, no top names would consent to appear in two-reelers, and so he had to content himself with stars who still had some name value, but who had slipped or were at least in temporary doldrums as a result of bad pictures or ill health. Thus he signed such stars as Lionel Barrymore, Priscilla Dean and Herbert Rawlinson for his comedies. The results were usually awkward, less funny than usual, and sometimes rather embarrassing in their revelations of a star obviously down on his or her luck. At one time Roach even tried to get the great D. W. Griffith, who was going through the doldrums too, to direct some two-reelers. But of course Griffith would have none of that. However, this was Roach's only serious mistake. His comedies were more carefully planned than Sennett's, and the care showed. Sophisticated directors like Leo McCarey, F. Richard Jones and Charles Parrott (Charlie Chase) were more in evidence than straight slapstick directors. Roach certainly made his quota of slapstick, and good slapstick it was too. But violence, sight gags and chases were usually more solidly integrated into good story material and situational comedy than was the case with Sennett. Some of the best Roaches eschewed slapstick entirely in favor of wit and farce, and there are even some Laurel & Hardy comedies which contain but a single slapstick sight gag. Roach's role in establishing and perpetuating the Laurel & Hardy comedies can never be stressed enough.

The first, almost accidental, appearance together: from 1917's *Lucky Dog*.

The Modus Operandi

of LAUREL & HARDY

The Modus Operandi

of LAUREL & HARDY

Defining a comedian's appeal to his audience is not always easy, but one rule that seems to be a standard—certainly it applies to all the great comedians—is that they should subtly make themselves inferior to the audience, not so much in a sense of humility as in personal ability. We automatically take to our hearts characters in whom we can recognize much of ourselves, but of whom we can honestly say that we are a little bit smarter. Perhaps this is why the peak vogue for a brash, wisecracking, self-confident comedian like Bob Hope was comparatively brief, while the less spectacular popularity of Jack Benny, whose comedy was likewise verbal but more humble and self-effacing, has nevertheless been more constant. In Laurel & Hardy we can all recognize human failings that are not too exaggerated. Vanity tells us that we're not quite as dumb as Laurel and not quite as pompous as Hardy; but a slightly distorted honesty tells us that our friends and neighbors have exactly those failings. In laughing at Laurel & Hardy, we are affectionately laughing at our friends and ourselves, but from a safe and superior distance.

One can break down their appeal a little further. With certain comics—the Marx Brothers or W. C. Fields—there are no half-measures. One either reveres or detests them. Curiously, with Laurel & Hardy the division is rather different: One either adores or ignores them. They do not seem to inspire the re-

actions of intense antagonism that other highly specialized comedians do. Children seem to like and understand Laurel & Hardy best of all, perhaps because the two comedians are adults reacting to everything in a genuinely child-like manner. Men like Laurel & Hardy not just for their own sense of superiority, but for their virility and direct physical action in confronting everyday problems. Women, as a group, like Laurel & Hardy not at all. Asked why, they will usually dismiss them as "silly" and comment on the pain and cruelty in much of their slapstick. But this is undoubtedly a subterfuge, for women must sense the perennial battle against their sex that Laurel & Hardy carried on in their films. Few comedians have had the courage to use their leading ladies as anything but stock heroine-figures, lovely creatures to be protected, respected, even worshipped. True, Buster Keaton invariably made his heroines dumb, inefficient and tiresome. But despite his lack of sentimentality, he gave them a kind of automatic affection, as though they were too helpless to survive without it. Laurel & Hardy have been much more ruthless in their handling of womanhood —largely *American* womanhood, it might be added, although the motif has been retained in those few films that had foreign locales too. Only rarely have they given us a stock innocent heroine whom they champion in Chaplinesque fashion—and even then,

The Hal Roach Studios, birthplace of so much classic screen comedy.

as in *Way Out West, The Bohemian Girl* and *March of the Wooden Soldiers,* in such exaggerated form that it is clearly a contemptuous spoof. In *Any Old Port,* such a heroine, rescued from a brute of a guardian and an unwanted marriage, is not only a satirized figure, but in the fadeout turns out to be quite fickle anyway! But by far the majority of the Laurel & Hardy women fall into two other camps—the first includes the gold-digging Jezebel, the prostitute (explicit, if never actually so stated) without the heart of gold, the schemer who benefits from the boys' endeavors and then dumps them ungratefully, the crook or murderess, the gangster's mistress, roles played by a number of actresses but never better than by their frequent nemesis, Mae Busch; the other category we can loosely but accurately define as "the wives." It is undoubtedly this latter category which has done the most to prevent approval of Laurel & Hardy by The Women Of America. Even admitting the frustrations and difficulties of living with Mr. Laurel & Mr. Hardy, this is a sore-headed, shrewish, grasping bunch; forever snapping, shouting, nagging, domineering, hoarding every dollar, begrudging their husbands an occasional night out, settling arguments amid a shower of pots, pans, vases hurled with unerring accuracy, rolling pins and shotguns, these latter apparently being a standard implement in the American Home, along with the walking stick and the umbrella. These wives are on the offensive even without provocation, and one recalls a delightful breakfast-table sequence in *Thicker Than Water* in which all's right with Hardy's world. The sun is shining, he is happy, the breakfast is to his liking,

and to show his appreciation of the little woman, he pays her a flowery compliment, puckers his lips into a kiss, and transfers that kiss to his spouse with an eloquent gesture of his forefinger. In mid-table, and without looking up from what she is doing, Mrs. Hardy intercepts the loving finger and bites it with a resounding crunch!

To make matters worse, Hardy's screen wives are not physical ogres, and are of smaller and slimmer build than he—especially in the case of diminutive Daphne Pollard, literally half his size. Laurel was rarely married in their comedies, his role being that of the best friend whom Mrs. Hardy hates with venomous passion. In the few films where he was married, his comparative bliss (achieved by passive non-resistance to his dominating spouse) was merely used as counterpoint to stress the futility of Hardy's attempts to be the boss in his own household. Small wonder then that the ladies have always liked Laurel & Hardy (and W. C. Fields) least of all the comedians, and Charlie Chaplin the most—at least until *Monsieur Verdoux*!

In constructing their films, Laurel & Hardy used a very simple modus operandi, depending far more on situation than on plot. Like children with a set of building blocks, they'd take a single idea, and on its base build mathematically and precisely, sometimes allowing themselves to shoot off on a tangent, but never swerving from a pre-determined destination. Very often their comedies would start off with two consecutive sequences intended as the overall structure, only to find that they could extract so much comedy from the first situation that they never even

28

needed the second. Thus, *A Perfect Day,* was intended to show the frustrations and delays in setting off in their car for a picnic, with the picnic itself planned as the climactic third of the film. But so many gags came out of the preparation of sandwiches, the frayed tempers, the problems of fitting a gout-afflicted Edgar Kennedy into their car, the avoiding of the local minister (it is a Sunday, of course), encounters with irate neighbors and prolonged farewells to friendly ones, that when the balky old automobile finally does come to life and depart for the picnic, it only has time to round a corner and settle gracefully beneath the murky waters of a gigantic mudpuddle before the "End" title appears. This ultra-painstaking "milking" of every gag and the precise—sometimes *too* precise—construction was one of the prime virtues of the Laurel & Hardy films, but at times also one of their greatest drawbacks. When the method worked, and it usually did, it gave audiences the joy of *anticipating* a gag far in advance. When the gag finally arrived, it usually more than lived up to expectations, or perhaps presented a neat and unexpected twist in execution, so that familiarity, amazingly, never bred boredom or anticlimaxes, On the other hand, in those films where their material was below par, or the directorial pacing was off, this same kind of construction would produce exasperating slowness and heavy-handedness, and the films were lucky indeed to have the physical presences of Laurel & Hardy, for no other clowns could do so much with so little.

Two unique comedy motifs have always dominated the Laurel & Hardy films, the most spectacular of these being the now-familiar sado-masochistic exchanges of savage, yet well-ordered and almost "civilized," violence. For an argument which may be either a climactic wrap-up or a carefully built orgy which consumes the entire running time, Laurel & Hardy, solidly united for once, square off for battle against an opponent who is usually James Finlayson, he of the bald head, pickle-shaped nose, and walrus moustache, or small and apparently mild-mannered Charles Hall. The argument, of course, starts over nothing at all; a misunderstanding, an imagined insult, a pure accident. The initial blow is merely a mild chastisement, designed to put an immediate end to the bothersome business; but the retaliatory gesture is stronger and more painful, and demands a correspondingly more powerful comeback. And thus it builds with a kind of businesslike and casual sadism, slap followed by kick, a tie amputated just be-

Hal Roach, producer, occasionally writer or director, and creator of the team of Laurel & Hardy.

low the knot succeeded by a shirt ripped up the back, a poke in the eye supplemented by the yanking of a handful of hair, and when all the physical indignities have been disposed of, then the offensive is changed to personal property. Starting with the wrecking of a watch, nothing is spared until the orgy of destruction has expended its fury, and with automobile, home, store and business all totally demolished, nothing is left for the opponents to do but patch it all up, proclaim a truce, and scheme some little wrap-up indignity that will give at least one of them a face-saving final victory. The beauty of all these exchanges is in their rich contrast of savage temper explosions with calm and orderly reasoning processes. It is one of the rules of the game that the victim make no move to protect himself or his property. As Hardy delicately pours a large bottle of sticky syrup all over the money in Charlie Hall's cash register, or deliberately lifts a large barrel of lard over Hall's head and then rams it home, Hall waits and suffers silently and stoically, almost as interested in what is going to happen to him next as are his tormenters. He knows full well that it will be his turn in a moment, and that Laurel & Hardy in a like sportsmanly manner, with submit passively to whatever he has to offer.

The second, subtler, less spectacular but probably even more effective gambit in their comedy stockpile is Hardy's stare, or direct appeal to the audience. It predates, and in any case far transcends, those now overly-familiar gags of the Bob Hope and *Hellzapoppin'* genre, in which on-screen characters converse with the audience, or toss off wisecracks about the movie itself. Importantly, Hardy never speaks a word to the audience. He thus never comes *out* of the picture, but rather invites the audience to join him *in* it. In moments of despair and hopelessness, after having been on the receiving end of some particularly spectacular ineptitude from Laurel, he turns that chubby face directly to the camera, a resigned shrug of the shoulders, a helpless widening of the eyes, as much in disbelief as in outrage, and a martyred sigh, literally asking the audience to spare him the compassion and understanding he needs so badly, and by sharing his burden to lighten it. The same stare also tells audiences that they have been through it all with him before so many times that they, like him, must have become fatalistically resigned to living with misfortune. Once in a while Hardy would vary the routine slightly, to the extent of taking the audience into his confidence, sharing his doubts, and letting the audience "sweat it out" with him as a particular piece of business unfolded. But even here the rapport with the other side of the screen was done entirely via eloquent but entirely mute pantomime. The wisdom of such an approach is certainly borne out by the durability of the gag, for never in the two decades of its use did it ever become tiresome or lose its freshness. Conversely, the vocal as well as visual direct contact with the audience in *Tom Jones,* effective the first time it was used, became merely precious and boring when it was repeated a second and a third time.

In addition to the violence of the mutually-destructive bouts already discussed, the infliction of pain, often in a physically repellent manner, was very much a part of their comic arsenal. Pain, alas, *can* be very funny—to the non-injured party—and Laurel & Hardy realized this very quickly. But they also saw that, in movie terms, pain is funniest when it is clearly an illusion. Thus neither they nor their opponents are ever really hurt, despite the most appalling misfortunes, and although clever editing and con-

LAUREL & HARDY

struction often suggests otherwise, the *act* of inflicting pain itself is usually only suggested in their comedies. A classic example: In *The Music Box,* Hardy is bent low, out of camera range, behind a crate. Laurel enters from the left of screen, carrying a ladder. One end of the ladder disappears into the area where Hardy is concealed; a dull thud and an agonized howl tells us that contact has been made; and Hardy rises majestically into view, hand nursing and covering a presumably all-but-demolished eye! Sadism worked and was funny in their silent comedies because the very absence of sound created an unreal fantasy world, in which one could accept a man's being kicked off a high cliff, landing on his head, getting up and nonchalantly strolling away, merely because seeing was believing and there were no sounds from the realistic outside world to shatter our belief in what we saw. That is why Harold Lloyd climbing his buildings in *Safety Last,* a silent, is so much funnier and more effective than Harold Lloyd doing exactly the same in a talkie, *Feet First.* In the latter, we are suddenly in a *real* world — we hear Lloyd's gasps of exertion and his desperate cries for help; the muffled street noises constantly remind us how far he has to fall, and of the very real danger he faces. Consequently the humor of the situation lessens, even if the excitement quotient rises proportionately. Laurel & Hardy, however, used sound creatively, to maintain and extend their fantasy world. Thus, when Hardy hits Laurel on the head with a heavy wrench, we hear the sound of a great bell reverberating in an empty echo chamber. When Hardy is blown up by his gas stove or takes a mighty tumble downstairs, the actual moment of impact takes place off-screen, the sound track enhancing its comedy value with exaggerated effects which make a simple fall sound like the San Francisco earthquake. The two comedians were also fond of literally repulsive fadeout gags which found them in a state of physical distortion. Throughout *The Live Ghost,* Walter Long threatens to twist their necks "so that when you're walking North you'll be looking south," and of course in the last scene does just that. In a probable take-off on Tod Browning's *Freaks,* they once wound up sitting on a sofa, their arms and legs literally tied in knots. And on another occasion Laurel, hiding in a barrel of water, drinks it all and emerges as a waddling giant balloon of a man. Such bizarre gags are made even more surrealistic by their sound effects of bones being crunched, and bodies

VS. THE WIVES

being pummelled and twisted. "Black" humor is rampant in most of the Laurel & Hardy films; when sickness is part of the plot (as in *Laughing Gravy*) it is invariably something rather loathsome like small-pox; when in that same film Charlie Hall takes his gun and goes off screen to commit suicide, we hear not one but *two* evenly spaced reports; bumps on the head grow to astronomical proportions, and when Hardy falls into a rain barrel, it is invariably covered with thick ice, so that he has to remove the broken chunks before he can escape from his predicament. When they turn in for the night, fleas share

The mute appeal for audience sympathy.

their bed. A wedding cake is covered with noisy flies, which Laurel assassinates with Flit, not realizing that their carcasses will remain in the icing. And even for the time-honored fall into the bathtub, the bath water contrives to look incongruously filthy. All these elements are never stressed by Laurel & Hardy, however. They are merely used as casual punctuation, so that while black humor is a constant in their work, what we now term "sick" humor never was.

There seems to have been no rule of thumb in determining which of their films turned out as masterpieces and which disappointed. Some of the films with the most promising concepts turned out to be among their weakest efforts, while others which must have seemed run-of-the-mill in script or story-board form emerged as classics. Certainly their directors seemed to have little to do with their successes or failures. Like Harold Lloyd, they never actually directed their own films, but they controlled them every foot of the way, and directed their directors. Only once—on the feature *Sons of the Desert*—did they encounter a director who seemed to have a perfect rapport with their style and who was able to build on and expand what they brought to the film. Curiously, this director was William Seiter, a master of tasteful family comedies, but hardly the kind of film-maker one would expect to be an ideal mentor for purveyors of a very different kind of comedy. Unfortunately, he made no other films with them. Their other di-

rectors ranged from hacks to genuine craftsmen, and the skills of the directors often seemed quite unrelated to the merits of the films. In other words, some of the best Laurel & Hardy films were made by mediocre directors—and some of their weakest by the "best" directors. Working with them had spectacular effects on the style of at least one director. James Horne, a director of sophisticated comedies and melodramas in the 20's, joined them at the end of the silent period, made some of their very best silent and sound comedies (including those enduring classics, *Big Business* and *Way Out West*), and thereafter seemed unable to take *any* films seriously. Directing serials for Columbia in the early 40's, he paced them like comedies, and had heroes and villains alike engage in the kind of florid gestures, stares at the audience, and exaggerated reaction shots that had hitherto been the domain of Oliver Hardy and James Finlayson. Incredibly, nobody seemed to know what he was doing. Perhaps the studio heads never bothered to screen his serials—or the more sober ones directed by men like Lambert Hillyer. Seen today, Horne's serials are wild and delightful forays into near-insanity, and have the same spirit of fun and comic violence that he brought to his Laurel & Hardy shorts and features.

There is no clear-cut dividing line between the silent and the sound comedies of Laurel & Hardy. Even after they had made their first talkie they made

The *anticipated* gag: Seconds before a mighty dive, Hardy contemptuously tells Stan, *"I'll* take it; you might *spill* it!"

a number of silents, some of which were those hybrid films designed for both silent release (with titles) and sound release (with limited dialogue and sound effects). Films thus designed for two markets, and in a sense for two different media, were never wholly successful in either, and the Laurel & Hardy comedies in that category were no exception, often seeming clumsy and faltering. But no comics made the precarious transfer from silents to sound with more ease and assurance than Stan and Ollie; it was necessary to change neither their screen images nor the basic pattern of their films. It's true that the bulk of their really creative work had been done in the last three years of the silent cinema and that their talkies were largely reworkings of their silent gags and in some cases exact remakes of whole subjects. But sound did bring a whole new range to their comedy, particularly in the case of Hardy, whose eloquent and grandiose posturings of gallantry and courtesy—a façade made the more effective by the reduced circumstances his plots placed him in, and the shabby clothes he wore—could now be further punctuated by dialogue. The strange cameraderie between the two boys (basically they like and are devoted to each other, despite Hardy's bullying and a selfishness that usually escapes his dull-witted cohort) could be far more subtly explored in exchanges of dialogue. A whole new array of catch-phrases came into being from the lips of Mr. Hardy: the resigned *"Another fine mess you've gotten me into!"*, the plaintive "Why don't you do something to *help* me?", the half-

apologetic "This is my friend, Mr. Laurel." The Laurel & Hardy talkies are full of glorious small talk, and many of the lines have the same kind of surrealistic absurdity as the visual gags. Answering the phone in *Going Bye Bye,* Hardy bids the caller hold on a moment with "Pardon me just a moment, my ear is full of milk!"—an explanation that in the context of the film makes perfect sense. Only the deliberate "joke lines" seem to fall flat in their movies; Laurel & Hardy are humanly and inherently funny in themselves, so alien to the field of stand-up comics that "one-liners" seem forced and heavy in their hands.

Sound also gave the boys added props for their sight gags; apart from its contribution to the gags of violence, already covered, sound was often used to punctuate a deliberately unreal visual gag. One of the most oft-used gags was for Hardy to fall below the frame line into the ocean or a pond. An unnaturally long pause or a slowly diminishing cry from Hardy would stress the dizzy depths of the fall. Then a very loud off-screen splash, followed by the deliberately unconvincing arrival of the water on screen —quite clearly the work of two handymen just throwing a couple of buckets of water from behind the cameras. There was a similar almost contemptuous laziness present in the musical scores of the films too; some half-dozen catchy but rather shapeless themes were used constantly and repetitiously throughout all their talkies. Even when a radio was turned on or a phonograph record was played, one of these

The orderly exchanges of violence: James Finlayson's home is wrecked in *Big Business;* and an altercation between Laurel & Hardy, Charlie Hall and a recalcitrant gum machine in *Two Tars*.

themes would surely emerge. However, "The Cuckoos," the theme music utilized for the main titles of the Laurel & Hardy films and often for their initial appearance within the film, was a genuinely inspired musical choice.

If one has any overall complaint to make concerning Laurel & Hardy, it is only that they were far too complacently aware of their limitations, or at least of the boundaries of their own world. The only experimental searching for a change of pace is to be

With pert Marion Byron, leading lady comedienne in several Roach comedies.

found in their earliest films together. For the rest of their career they were content to rework, to polish, to perfect, but never to explore. In one sense they may have been wise. The least successful comedies of Buster Keaton and Harry Langdon were those in which they tried to be radically different. Perhaps Laurel & Hardy's complacency was occasioned by the fact that they were never fully appreciated by the critics, and thus, unlike Chaplin, Keaton and Langdon, had no intellectual reputation to live up to, and to try to improve on. Certainly Chaplin's initial "expansion" due to critical lionizing produced a retrogression, his First Nationals being far inferior to the Mutuals that preceded them, although in time, of course, he more than justified himself. But Laurel & Hardy were never faced with such prodding or stimulation, and while limiting themselves so severely produced some masterpieces of organized simplicity, it also meant that they had no qualms about accepting the second-rate at times. But second-rate Laurel & Hardy is still a good deal better than first-rate almost anybody else. It would be unfair even to consider their last film, *Atoll K,* as an unsuccessful attempt to experiment, since it came too late to be considered part of the main body of their work or for it to have had much effect on films they might subsequently have made. But it can perhaps be taken as an indication that their own familiar little world was the best of all worlds for them, and that we should after all be grateful that they never tried to change or intellectualize it.

The Films
of LAUREL & HARDY

The Films of
LAUREL & HARDY

The list that follows concerns itself only with the films that Laurel & Hardy made together, first as contract players for Hal Roach and then as a co-starring team. However, the three films in which Hardy later appeared without Laurel are referred to in passing. After their teaming, Laurel appeared in no films without Hardy, although he was the nominal producer of a series of "B" musical Westerns in the mid-30's, and the actual producer, in conjunction with Hal Roach, of one of his features. Previous at-

tempts to compile a definitive list of their shorts have contained some understandable errors, due primarily to their appearance in pre-starring days in a series that Hal Roach somewhat loosely termed the "Comedy All Star" series. While they did appear either separately or as a team in many of these, they were by no means in all of them. *Should Tall Men Marry?*, a 1927 two-reeler invariably listed as a Laurel & Hardy subject, actually features Laurel only, together with Theodore Van Eltz and Stuart Holmes. The inclusion of *Eve's Love Letters* in the listing of their films is likewise a pardonable error, especially since Hardy may well have been intended for the film at one time. Indeed, a supporting player at one point profers his card, which identifies him as one Oliver N. Hardy! Perhaps because its title brings to mind sequences in two other Laurel & Hardy silents, *Liberty* and *You're Darn Tootin'*, Charlie Chase's *The Way of All Pants* is likewise frequently referred to as a Laurel & Hardy comedy. Finally, many Sennetts of the mid-20's—*Circus Today, The Daredevil,* and others—are frequently credited to Oliver Hardy, even though he is not in them. The confusion can usually be traced to the fact that a Sennett comedian, Kewpie Morgan, who bore a striking resemblance to Hardy both in face and in figure, *was* in them. Hardy's appearance under the Sennett banner were sparse indeed, totalling but a half-dozen films over a ten-year period, the last of them being a 1925 beach comedy in which he played a movie director.

Cast listings on many of the Laurel & Hardy shorts are brief, not because the information is unavailable, but because they worked with a small stock company of players and because their plots—simple and restricted—often involved no more than two or three characters in addition to themselves. Insofar as production credits are concerned, producer, director, writer and cameraman are listed for all the features. In the case of the many shorts however, usually only the director is listed. Scenarios as such were almost non-existent on many of their shorts, although a great deal of credit for pungent sub-titles and basic story ideas goes to one of the most valuable members of their team, H. M. Walker. Script and photography credits are supplied on their shorts only when such information has historical interest,

inasmuch as several creative film-makers got their start with Laurel & Hardy.

Laurel & Hardy stills have a very happy knack of being entirely representative of the films they illustrate. Even the posed stills, sometimes unavoidable when publicity shots cannot be taken during shooting, eschew the common practice of arranging all the players in as many comic and slapsticky positions as possible, regardless of relevance to the picture. Laurel & Hardy stills invariably tell a story in themselves and, as in the actual films, it is the expressions and attitudes of their faces and bodies, in response to a clearly shown situation, that provokes the laughter. Selecting from a set of Laurel & Hardy stills is a frustrating experience, since there are never any wasted shots, no pointless mugging closeups. In fact, full portraits of the stars are in a striking minority. Some of their lesser films have a habit of looking hilarious just from the stills, while the great films—*Two Tars,* for example—offer such a rich array of stills that they almost demand a chapter to themselves! One extremely valuable function that the stills perform, too, is to record (since in many cases the film is long since gone) at least some of the many sequences that Laurel & Hardy shot and never included in their films. Some of these sequences look wildly bizarre, even near-surrealist, and one must assume that they were cut only because their inclusion would have disrupted the simple and well-organized continuity upon which the comedians finally decided. A filmic compilation of these discarded episodes would be a real treasure trove, but since such a possibility is very remote, we have done the next best thing by including at the end of this volume a brief but representative collection of stills from these lost comic gems.

Forty-Five Minutes from Hollywood

HAL ROACH–PATHE, 1926.

Important only as being probably the first Hal Roach two-reeler in which both Laurel and Hardy appeared. A hodge-podge of a film, set largely in a Hollywood hotel, containing chunks of stock footage from earlier Roach comedies, and presenting the traditionally crazy picture of 1920's Hollywood, complete even to dinosaurs roaming the hills, it had speed, variety, and not much else. Just about all the Roach contract players except Charley Chase appeared in it, many in fleeting single shots. Laurel, curiously, was made up with an enormous moustache as an exact double for Jimmy Finlayson!

Duck Soup

HAL ROACH–PATHE, 1927. *Two reels.*

Unavailable in recent years for reappraisal, *Duck Soup* was a rather frenetically paced and unsubtle comedy, with Hardy's footage severely limited. Possibly its main distinctions are that part of it formed the basis for *Another Fine Mess,* one of the team's talkies, and that it was adapted from a sketch written by Stan Laurel's father.

Slipping Wives

HAL ROACH–PATHE, 1927. *Two reels. Directed by Fred Guiol. Supervised by F. Richard Jones. Camera: George Stevens.*
  Starring Priscilla Dean, with Herbert Rawlinson, Stan Laurel, Oliver Hardy, Albert Conti.

Neglected wife Priscilla Dean is determined to make husband Herbert Rawlinson jealous, and to this end conspires with handyman Stan Laurel to flirt with her in front of him. A guest at their weekend party, Laurel is introduced as a literary genius—an illusion he soon dispells—and to add to the confusion, mistakes another guest as the husband, thus performing all his flirting at the wrong time. After a wild midnight chase through the bedrooms, during the course of which Laurel is at one time caught, quite innocently, in bed with the wife, the husband learns the truth and Laurel goes on his way.

Not a very good comedy, and given to too much frenetic running around and pratfalls in the Sennett tradition, *Slipping Wives* is interesting in that it shows Laurel & Hardy almost automatically working together in sight gags, even though the roles are not written with teamwork in mind. Laurel first appears at the front door, a title informing us that he is "... out of the nowhere ... going nowhere ... delivering paint." Hardy is the family butler: dignified, aloof, hair smarmed down with Vaseline, and minus his moustache. Within seconds of his having opened the door to Laurel, they are grappling; the paint falls to the floor, Hardy expectedly nose-dives into it, and follows through with his piteous glance direct to the audience. Certainly an auspicious and typical start to years of teamwork! Laurel's role throughout is by far the bigger of the two, however, and his highlight is a superb piece of sustained visual pantomime as he acts out the story of Samson and Delilah, playing both parts and being especially amusing in the scenes of Samson's awakening and discovery of his missing hair. This sequence also contains some typical gleeful Laurel sadism, as he stumbles over invisible bodies and acts out the gouging of Samson's eyes, an operation apparently performed with a corkscrew.

The title-writing throughout is rather heavy-handed and below the standard of the visual comedy, which also includes such standbys-to-be as Hardy's attempt to give Laurel a bath and winding up, fully clothed, in the tub himself.

The subject was remade as a talkie by Laurel & Hardy under the title *The Fixer-Uppers,* reshaped of course to give them more prominence and its comedy content slower in pace and much subtler, but the basic plot and many of the gags remained unchanged.

Love 'Em and Weep

HAL ROACH–PATHE, 1927. *Two reels. Directed by Fred Guiol.*

With Stan Laurel, James Finlayson, Mae Busch, Oliver Hardy, Charlotte Mineau, Vivien Oakland, Charlie Hall.

Jimmy Finlayson, newly-married businessman, is unexpectedly visited in his office by gold-digging old flame Mae Busch, who has an old snapshot with which she is threatening blackmail. The new Mrs. Finlayson enters the office, and Mae is hurriedly hidden in the bathroom. Mae seems about to be discovered when the wife announces, "I must wash my hands—I had to change a tire," but Jimmy's fainting spell distracts his wife momentarily, who then discovers Mae's ermine fur. To placate his wife and get rid of her, Jimmy pretends that it is a present for her.

The wife gone, Mae demands the return of the fur, threatening to descend on the Finlayson household and tell all. Stan Laurel, Finlayson's business associate, is assigned the task of keeping Mae occupied and away from the house—a task not at all to Stan's liking, since he too has a suspicious wife. Of course, the best-laid schemes go awry, Mae arrives at the house during a party, and Stan is obliged to pretend that she is his wife. When his wife turns up, there are no further explanations or alibis possible, and the film finishes with the two husbands being beaten by their grim and unforgiving wives.

This was Laurel & Hardy's first concentrated foray into the terrifying world of women, and the film offers three nagging and suspicious wives, a money-grubbing ex-girl friend, and a harridan of a gossip! Hardy, billed fourth and disguised beneath sideburns, bushy moustache and thick glasses, had little to do as a guest at the party other than react to the troubles of others and finally to be set upon by *his* wife. The titles are amusingly written, and the best running gag has Laurel repeatedly being spotted by the gossip in dubious circumstances with Mae Busch. In one of these moments, he is wrestling with her on the sidewalk, and with great presence of mind, suggests that it is all a game. As she rushes away in her car, he leaps into his car, re-emerges with golf clubs, hits an imaginary ball far into the distance, and then is whisked away by his car in pursuit of it. Other typical gags: Laurel backing into a jalopy and demolishing it; Finlayson hurriedly sitting down on an incriminating framed photograph, and painfully removing huge slivers of glass from his rear end; and an ingenious bit of pantomime when Mae Busch has fainted, and Finlayson, bent double, supports her fur-coated body on his back while Stan leads his swaying and "inebriated" bride to the door.

The basic story was used again by Laurel & Hardy in their talkie *Chickens Come Home,* with Hardy in the Finlayson role and Laurel repeating as his far-from-helpful aide.

Why Girls Love Sailors

HAL ROACH–PATHE, 1927. *Two reels. Directed by Fred Guiol.*
With Stan Laurel and Oliver Hardy.

Laurel's beautiful young girl friend is kidnapped by burly sea captain Hardy and, in order to rescue her, Stan masquerades as a bejeweled vamp. Hardy flirts outrageously with his new conquest, only to be discovered by the customarily belligerent Mrs. Hardy, allowing Stan to escape with his girl.

A short that has apparently long since disappeared, *Why Girls Love Sailors* was important at least in Hardy's eyes, for in John McCabe's biography of the two comedians, *Mr. Laurel and Mr. Hardy,* he is quoted as crediting this film with the inadvertent discovery of the "tie twiddle," that wonderful piece of business that Ollie was to use so frequently to cover embarrassment and discomfort. However, Hardy also credits the "long stare" as originating in this film, and while it may have been *developed* in this film, the recognizable embryo of it can certainly be seen in earlier ones.

With Love and Hisses

HAL ROACH–PATHE, 1927. *Two reels. Directed by Fred Guiol.*
With Stan Laurel, Oliver Hardy, James Finlayson.

Almost plotless, this film was merely the standard succession of "awkward squad" and other Army gags.

Although slight and obvious, this film takes on some importance as being the first film in which the two comics worked together as a planned, rather than an accidental, team. As two raw recruits they are pitted against James Finlayson, their superior officer and automatic enemy, in a series of violent sight gags which form a kind of loose blueprint for the Laurel & Hardy-Finlayson battles to come. The film also contains a certain amount of homosexual humor (prevalent at the time through all silent comedy) and one good sight gag involving a huge poster for Cecil B. DeMille's *The Volga Boatman,* which, also being a Pathé release, was thus given a good free plug.

Sailors Beware

HAL ROACH–PATHE, 1927. *Two reels. Directed by Fred Guiol.*
With Stan Laurel, Oliver Hardy, Anita Garvin, Tiny Sanford, Viola Ritchard, Lupe Velez.

Laurel is a rather dim-witted cab driver, taking Anita Garvin and her infant son to the docks. The "infant," however, is actually a midget, disguised in order to work their card-sharping and jewelry thieving rackets aboard ship. Accidentally, Stan and his cab are put on the ship and he promptly runs afoul of a rough-neck captain and his purser (Oliver Hardy). Put to work as a steward, Stan creates havoc among the passengers as he performs his new duties, but is redeemed and finds himself the hero of the hour when he discovers the true identity of the "baby" and returns the stolen loot. However, Hardy's stock with the ladies spirals down when, for the fadeout, he is beaten up by the midget.

Although reverting to their pre- *With Love and Hisses* status and not working as a team, Laurel & Hardy get almost equal footage (Laurel's is the greater by a small margin) and share the best gags evenly.

Lupe Velez (center) was an extra just on the brink of stardom when she made this short.

Hardy scores once again with his facial pantomime, especially in his first sequence (establishing him as a ladies' man), in which he checks the passengers' names as they enter the gangway. To the ladies he is charming and courteous, all smiles and pleasantries as he strives to make an instantly favorable impression; to the men he is surly, pushing them roughly aboard so that he can get to the next lady! Laurel's highlight is likewise one of facial pantomime, wherein he becomes involved in a game of dice with the bonnetted and diapered "baby," first just to humor him, and then with dawning apprehension and suspicions as he loses time and time again to the baby's skill and is unable to persuade him to return his losses. Later, still confused but as yet unaware that the baby is really an adult, he is asked by the mother to carry the baby down a long flight of stairs—and in pique and a sudden desire for revenge, he hurls the baby carriage, infant inside, down the stairs. Baby emerges rattled but unhurt, uttering an epithet (easily lip-read) which fortunately is not heard by the outraged onlookers. The baby's downfall finally comes when Laurel is ordered to give him a bath, and the infant is revealed to be the possessor of a very hairy chest.

While too much of the film is devoted to standard fast knockabout—chases and falls in the corridors, slapstick in and around the ship's swimming pool—nevertheless the bits of business and Laurel & Hardy mannerisms are becoming more frequent and more polished. Another major asset of this short (and of many later Laurel & Hardy comedies) is Anita Garvin, a statuesque, goodlooking and (in this film at least, thanks to provocative costuming) sexy girl, whose stock in trade was aggressive determination and the maintenance of icy dignity at all times, regardless of the calamities that might befall her.

Do Detectives Think?

HAL ROACH–PATHE, 1927. *Two reels. Directed by Fred Guiol.*

With Stan Laurel, Oliver Hardy, James Finlayson, Noah Young.

Convicted murderer Noah Young escapes from prison, vowing vengeance on the judge (James Finlayson) who sentenced him. Laurel & Hardy, inept employees of a private detective agency, are assigned to guard him. Waylaying the judge's new butler, the killer gets into his house in that guise. Prowling the house with huge knives and swords, Young misses several opportunities to kill his intended prey, and adds the detectives to his list of victims when they continually get in his way. Eager only to avoid him, and by now totally unconcerned by their mission to protect the judge, the boys do, by a fluke, capture him after all and after turning him over to the law, leave, bowing modestly and gracefully as they exit.

The first film to present Laurel & Hardy as the team we now know so well, it introduces them as already-established workmates, clothes them in their traditional bowler hats and rather shabby suits, and gives them their head to perform as though they had been a team for years. Hardy is pompous, selfish, scared, a blusterer; Laurel is well-meaning, dumb, equally scared, seldom aware of when he is being used by his buddy. Several of their standard routines originate here, including their many-times-repeated exchange of hats (the hats are continually dropped, picked up, passed from hand to hand, always resulting in the wrong hat on the wrong head). Although a disappointing comedy, it is an important one in that it offers their comedy style and screen personalities in full fruition (albeit served by inferior material), the two of them working together in perfect unison and harmony after only a handful of trial balloons which had made no deliberate attempt to create such a team. The film is further helped by considerably upped production values—handsome interior sets, a generous supply of crowd players in the opening courtroom sequence, and first-class camerawork. This latter is especially apparent in a well-designed graveyard sequence (obviously shot at night and not in the daytime with filters, as is the common practice) in which the boys are scared by their own exaggerated shadows, which seem to clutch at them from behind the tombstones. In escaping from the cemetery, the boys use a treadmill to create an illusion of greater speed,

For the first time, the two comedians introduce their standard costumes, topped by bowler hats.

the kind of mechanical aid to a gag which they rarely found necessary thereafter.

In view of the added care that went into the production of *Do Detectives Think?*, it is a pity that it isn't nearly as good as one would like the first authentic Laurel & Hardy vehicle to be. It contains entirely too much scared reaction comedy, running around, pratfalls, and such old mechanical gags as a grotesque mask improbably falling on to the back of the head of one of the participants (Finlayson) while he is wearing a sheet, thus provoking much frenetic running around in the belief that he is a genuine ghost. The best gags, other than the carefully worked out graveyard sequence, are almost throwaways: Finlayson as the judge, sentencing the fearsome killer to death and then, with a pop-eyed grimace, adding, "And I hope you choke!"; Laurel pouncing on the struggling figures of Hardy and the killer, and triumphantly placing the handcuffs on a pair of hands that of course turn out to be Hardy's; and Laurel proudly marching the finally subdued maniac into a closet, the briefly opened door showing us the sudden realization and terror on the face of Hardy, hiding within. Another worthwhile gag has Finlayson hiding submerged in the waters of his bath, while the maniac prowls the bathroom searching for him. Accidentally, Finlayson's foot removes the plug, and the water drains out—incidentally leaving a spectacularly dirty ring around the bathtub!

Although this film was never officially remade, many of the gags and specific situations in *Do Detectives Think?* were re-used by the comedians in later films, with *Going Bye Bye* being the most obvious parallel.

46

Edna Marion (with Hardy) and Dorothy Coburn (with Laurel) as stone-age flappers.

Flying Elephants

HAL ROACH—PATHE, 1927. *Two reels. Directed by Frank Butler.*

With Stan Laurel, Oliver Hardy, James Finlayson, Viola Ritchard, Tiny Sanford, Leo Willis.

It is the Stone Age, and the King decrees that all bachelors must marry immediately, on pain of death or banishment, or both. Hardy, a worldly-wise warrior, and Laurel, a virginal young man, both take a shine to the same attractive Stone-Ager, the daughter of James Finlayson, whose normal sour disposition is heightened by an outsize toothache. After some rather indecisive contests to prove their athletic and hunting skills, Laurel takes Hardy to the top of a cliff, intending to kill him. His attempt misfires, but an irritated goat achieves what Laurel had failed to do, and Hardy is butted off the cliff, presumably to his death, and Laurel claims the girl.

Although made in late 1927, this comedy was not released until after Roach and Laurel & Hardy had moved to M-G-M, where their comedies took an immediate upswing. Thus audiences could hardly have been very satisfied with this loosely constructed farce in which the two comedians again performed as solo comedians, joining up for some brief teamwork only in the closing scenes of the film. Like Chaplin's *His Prehistoric Past,* it uses modern gags and slang idiom in a prehistoric period, and the con-trast just isn't as funny as it should be. (Chaplin's film turned out to be a dream at the end; Laurel & Hardy's doesn't.) Well photographed, partially in the same locations that Roach was to utilize in 1940 for his serious prehistoric essay, *One Million B.C., Flying Elephants* takes place entirely out-of-doors, and has the off-the-cuff look of many of the early Chaplin "park" comedies. Its best moments are little vignettes of individual pantomime from the two stars. Hardy swaggers in with his customary aplomb, wearing his stone-age furs and skins with the same dignity that he brought to equally ragged modern clothes. In up-to-date garb he'd smooth out a solitary wrinkle from a suit that was *all* wrinkles, and square his shoulders for the inevitable gesture of flinging back an invisible cloak. With leopard skin and club he is no less the poised man about town, beaming amiably as he searches for, finds, and flicks away, a speck on his war club. Laurel makes *his* entrance skipping gaily along the rocky rim of a cliff, effectively photographed in long-shot and semi-silhouette. His best sequence: an amusing fishing pantomime in which he wades into a stream, catches flies out of the air, carefully places them on the water, and then belts the fish with his club when they swallow the flies.

The barely relevant title comes from a typical piece of Hardy small talk, when he is commenting on the warm weather and pointing out that the elephants are flying south—while a trick shot shows us just that.

Sugar Daddies

HAL ROACH—M-G-M, 1927. *Director: Fred Guiol. Camera: George Stevens. Two reels.*

With James Finlayson, Stan Laurel, Oliver Hardy, Noah Young, Charlotte Mineau, Will Stanton, Edna Marion, Eugene Pallette.

James Finlayson, newly-rich oil tycoon, is wakened from his slumbers one morning by faithful butler Hardy, who casually reminds him that he was married the night before. Frantically, he calls his lawyer, Stan Laurel, for advice—and the mess never does really sort itself out, but the pursuit of a blackmailing ring makes for some lively slapstick and chase sequences in dance hall and amusement park.

A run-of-the-mill entry, *Sugar Daddies* is lively and fast, and though hardly inspired, gains immeasurably from the nostalgic and lengthy sequences set in an amusement park, with much of the action taking place on rides that have long since disappeared from the scene. Its best single gag is borrowed from *Love 'Em and Weep* from earlier that same year—with James Finlayson (again!) bent over double and Laurel, in yet another dame masquerade, perched uneasily on his shoulders. A cop, watching all of the mayhem, finally cottons to the deception but—having temporarily lost the Finlayson-Laurel "dame" in the crowd—picks on the wrong party to prove his keen powers of observation. Striding along, enjoying the sights, are Eugene Pallette and his wife. Triumphantly the cop pounces, and hoists high the lady's skirts . . . . at which point the two-reeler tactfully closes.

Call of the Cuckoo

HAL ROACH–M-G-M, 1927. *Two reels. Directed by Clyde Bruckman. Supervised by Leo McCarey.*
With Max Davidson, Specs O'Donnell, Laurel & Hardy, Charlie Chase, James Finlayson.

Max Davidson moves into his charming new house, which, alas, is far from being as substantial as it looks. Appliances fail to work, doors fall off, and while he is enjoying a bath on the floor above, the dirty bath water seeps through the floor into the soup of the

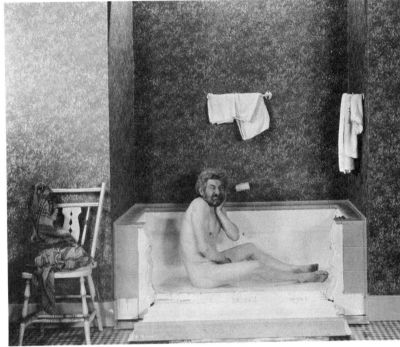

Believe it or not, this shot of Max Davidson in his collapsing bathtub *did* appear in the film!

dinner guests below! To further add to his embarrassment, the building immediately adjacent to his is an insane asylum, and inmates Laurel & Hardy, James Finlayson and Charlie Chase cavort on his lawn. Finally, since even his floor is not level, the piano glides majestically through the walls, carrying most of his dream house into the street.

The Davidson comedies were often tremendously funny, rich in both visual and situational gags, but they have seldom been revived because they are built

so much around Jewish stereotypes—albeit pleasant and inoffensively exaggerated ones. However, a representative cross-section of the Davidson humor was included in Robert Youngson's compilation *Laurel and Hardy's Laughing Twenties*. Laurel & Hardy (their heads shaved because of their convict roles in the concurrently filmed *The Second Hundred Years*) are merely guest stars here, playfully mugging and staging a mock William Tell act in a kind of home-movie atmosphere.

The Second Hundred Years

HAL ROACH—M-G-M, 1927. *Two reels. Directed by Fred Guiol. Story by Leo McCarey.*
With Laurel & Hardy, James Finlayson, Eugene Pallette, Tiny Sanford.

Laurel & Hardy are convicts, resigned to their fate but ever alert to opportunities for escape. A tunnel to freedom merely brings them out into the warden's office, but when two painters at work in the yard go off to lunch, the pair have a bright idea. Turning their coats inside out, they pick up the paint and brushes and walk out of the front gate. A suspicious cop follows them, and to prove that they *are* painters, they cover everything in sight with white paint. Needing clothes, they steal the elegant garb of two dignitaries and take their place in a limousine. Alas, their victims are French prison officials making a tour of inspection of the very prison from which Laurel & Hardy have just escaped. Back in their own prison, but as guests, the boys manage to keep up the deception through the elaborate luncheon that the warden has prepared for them. But on a tour of the cells, the *real* dignitaries are discovered—arrested for inde-

cent exposure—and so it's back behind the bars for the hapless couple, who accept it all in good spirit.

The first "official" Laurel & Hardy release, *The Second Hundred Years* was an excellent comedy in every way, and though it would be surpassed by a handful of genuine classics, it would always remain as one of the best of their second-echelon comedies. It stressed two things: 1. That Laurel & Hardy were the creative forces behind their own films and needed an "official" director mainly to perform a traffic-cop function and keep the production moving, for Fred Guiol who directed this particular film was a highly competent journeyman director at best, whose comedies away from Laurel & Hardy were seldom inspired; 2. That they were beginning to slow down the tempo of their comedies and concentrate far more on situation than on plot. *The Second Hundred Years* does fall back on one or two unlikely complications to "justify" the plot, but basically it is divided into three lengthy episodes, each of which is milked to the hilt and could play on its own as a separate comedy segment. As time went on, the comedians were to do away with plot "pegs" even more, and for the

The convicts, unwitting guests of the warden, do their best to conceal their lack of social graces.

most part reduce their "divisions" from three to two, and in many cases sustaining just one situation throughout an entire two-reeler.

The film starts out with deliberately minor gags. Laurel approaches a rough-looking convict and asks him when he'll be released. Dejectedly, the con tells Laurel that he's in for another thirty years. But Laurel is delighted, and gives him a letter with the request, "Mail this for me when you get out." The highlight of the film is the middle portion, when the boys escape from prison disguised as painters. At the gate, fear and the need for caution prevent their making a sudden bolt for it. Nonchalantly, they proceed to paint the gates and a small rock in the driveway. Their studied conscientiousness arouses the baffled suspicion of a typical Hal Roach policeman—one who is determined to be in possession of *all* the facts first, hesitates to make an arrest despite the most damning evidence and who, poker-faced, gives the boys all the rope they need to hang themselves. With him stalking a few steps behind them, the boys head for town and, with an inexhaustible supply of white paint in their small cans, proceed to prove that they are painters by daubing everything in sight — from the front of Ice Cream Cohen's parlor, to the windows, hood, and engine of a parked auto. Nimbly they skip

across a street, their brushes skipping over the white crossing lines that already exist. Despite sequences like this that built and built, chuckle rumbling into guffaw, guffaw exploding into belly-laugh, Laurel & Hardy were never at a loss for a quick and sure-fire payoff gag to wrap it all up with. In this instance, Laurel is busily painting a lamp post, and turns away for a moment to dip his brush once more. Down the street comes a charming, long-legged, tight-skirted flapper. Briefly she pauses by the lamp post to look into her pocket-mirror and preen herself before crossing the street. Her vanity is her undoing, for Laurel turns around to renew his assault on the lamp post, and promptly and energetically lays several layers of paint up and down, sideways and backwards, on the young lady's waiting derrière. The climactic luncheon not only gives warden James Finlayson some splendid opportunities for visual disbelief at the coarseness of his French guests' table manners, but also provides Laurel with a good routine as a cherry escapes from his fruit salad, and trying to maintain both aplomb and the best of etiquette, he pursues it around the table with a spoon. The routine was to be repeated, and polished still further, a scant half-dozen pictures later in *From Soup to Nuts*.

51

Hats Off

HAL ROACH—M-G-M, 1927. *Two reels. Directed by Hal Yates. Supervised by Leo McCarey.* *With Laurel & Hardy, Max Davidson.*

Handymen Laurel & Hardy have to deliver an awkward washing machine to a house at the top of a huge flight of steps.

One of the most frustrating items in the mercifully small list of missing Laurel & Hardy comedies, *Hats Off,* though made by a minor director, would be especially interesting and valuable to see again in that it is so obviously the source of inspiration for their Academy Award-winning sound classic, *The Music Box.* Even the same huge flight of stone steps seems to have been used as the location for the basic gag, although by the time of *The Music Box* the area had been built up rather more. *Hats Off,* which has a sequence in which a group of irate pedestrians converge in the middle of a street and, goaded into action by Laurel & Hardy, destroy each other's headgear, also was obviously a simple precursor of such films as *You're Darn Tootin'* and *Battle of the Century,* with their larger-scale episodes of similar mass hysteria.

It is strange indeed that by this period in 1927 Laurel & Hardy weren't already regarded as fairly big comedy stars. Anticipating that their box office stock would be boosted by the move to M-G-M, Pathé had held off releasing several of their Pathé two-reelers, and these now suddenly appeared at the same time as the initial M-G-M releases. Trade reviews were good, audience response enthusiastic. Yet M-G-M and Hal Roach still failed to recognize the goldmine they had. Shorts were of much greater importance in those days than today, and were advertised extensively in the trade press. Frequently, entire issues of trade magazines would be devoted entirely to short subjects. Yet, while M-G-M was not penny-pinching in its publicity, all of the big guns went to publicizing Charlie Chase, Max Davidson, and Our Gang. Even at the end of 1927, Laurel & Hardy were still represented in ads only by small individual photos of each player, with no indication even that they were a team. This odd situation recalls Metro's earlier failure to recognize the potential of Rudolph Valentino and their policy of continuing to give him non-starring roles (and little publicity) in a handful of films even after his overnight triumph in *The Four Horsemen of the Apocalypse.*

Putting Pants on Philip

HAL ROACH—M-G-M, 1927. *Two reels. Directed by Clyde Bruckman.*
With Laurel & Hardy, Harvey Clark.

J. Piedmont Mumblethunder (Hardy) waits at the dock to greet his nephew from Scotland, amused by the antics of a disembarking kilted nitwit (Laurel) who is too shy to allow the ship's doctor to see his vaccination, and pitying the poor fellow who has to collect him. To his horror, he soon realizes that *he* is the poor fellow, and does his best to (a) keep publicly disassociated from such a sorry spectacle, (b) try to replace the kilts with pants, and (c) keep his woman-crazy nephew from chasing every pair of flapper skirts in sight. On all three he counts, he fails spectacularly.

Made earlier and held out of release until the team's popularity was better established, *Putting Pants on Philip* is one of their finest comedies, though one that is often out of favor with the more rabid Laurel & Hardy devotees. For one thing, the characters play off and against each other rather than *with* each other; none of their regular cohorts (Kennedy, Finlayson, Charlie Hall, etc.) are involved; and the comedy is not *typical* Laurel & Hardy material, having overtones rather more of Keaton and W. C. Fields (with both of whom Clyde Bruckman, the director, was frequently associated). Further, the film has decided elements of homosexual humor, a spasmodically repeated gag motif in Laurel & Hardy comedies, and a motif which many of their admirers deny or repudiate as though it automatically indicates vulgarity, which of course it does not. *Putting Pants on Philip* scores on three levels: as a fine showcase for the contrasting pantomime of its stars; on its limited but first-rate sight gags; and on its design and construction as a comedy. Visually it is a model of intelligent and attractive screen comedy. Despite titles that are genuinely amusing, it can and does tell its whole story in subtly visual terms. One running gag deals with Laurel's impassioned pursuit of girls; and of the crowd's fascination by, and pursuit of, him. Thus at frequent intervals during the film, as the chase begins anew, the basic action is repeated, but

always with a fresh approach; here a direct statement and there a subtle suggestion; suddenly rushing feet glimpsed from a basement window, or heads all running in one direction, as seen from the top deck of a bus, all culminating in an overhead long shot of curious crowds surrounding Laurel in the middle of a street, a crowd that naturally gets bigger with each new climax. Obviously carefully pre-planned, all of this has a marvelously spontaneous feeling, and indeed some shots may well have been fortunate happenstance—for example, the little dog that suddenly takes after Hardy, snapping at his heels to add to his already considerable troubles.

Hardy's basic characteristics—geniality tempered

by pomposity—have seldom been better employed than in the sequences where he is escorting Laurel from the boat and down the street. He is too embarrassed to have a kilted freak walk side by side with him, and Laurel *will* keep catching up and linking arms. Hardy explains that he knows every man, woman and child in town; will Laurel *please* stay behind? And in long, smooth tracking shots through the streets of Culver City (then bright and prosperous looking, easily recognizable today, physically unchanged but somehow much seedier looking) Hardy strides along, a courtly greeting to a neighbor here, a beaming smile there, his straw hat perched so debonairly on his head and his jaunty swagger proclaiming to the world that he couldn't possibly be aware of, let alone know, the oddball trailing along behind him. Laurel walks over a ventilation grating, and his kilts billow upwards. Of course he is wearing natty shorts beneath, and of course it is but a setup for the obvious gag to come, a gag that gains by being anticipated. He pauses to take snuff, sneezes, and the shorts flutter to the ground. Unaware of his dilemma, Laurel strides on, over the next ventilation shaft. A quick shot establishing that the skirts are again flying up cuts immediately to a crowd reaction shot; two young ladies, horrified out of their wits, faint on the spot, their limp bodies supported by the crowd. The cop on the beat hurriedly informs Hardy that his pal "ain't got no lingerie on"; Laurel inspects himself curiously, and the gag continues with variations for a few moments, not trying to top that highlight, but deliberately tapering down to the next major bit of business. This is Hardy's attempt to get Laurel measured for, and put into, a nice respectable pair of pants. Laurel is shy and cautious; he *wants* to cooperate, but is terrified every time the tailor comes near him with the tape measure. Hardy talks to him soothingly, while the tailor sneaks up behind. But Laurel is on to their game, and begins to look on Hardy as a man who is betraying his trust. Finally, direct action is the only answer. Hardy takes off his coat, rolls up his sleeves, and plunges in. Laurel is subdued, and hauled off to a fate worse than death behind a curtain. After a sinister delay, pregnant with foreboding, the tailor reappears, nods affirmatively at Hardy, and jots down the critical measurement. Moments later Laurel reappears, clothing disarrayed, his face reflecting the resignation and despair of the seduced virgin, and after struggling for a moment to regain his composure, he gives up and bursts into tears.

It's a beautiful bit of pantomime, hilarious because of its absurdity and satire, faintly poignant because of its distant relation to truth. Wisely, the situation is *not* milked; the point is made, and the comedy moves briskly on to something else.

There have certainly been faster and funnier Laurel & Hardy comedies, but few that were so beautifully designed or so flawlessly edited. The cuts all come at such "right" moments that editorially it almost has the rhythm and precision of an Eisenstein or Griffith work. And just how much Laurel & Hardy benefited from creative and careful editing can be gauged from even a casual look at some of their earlier talkies—for example, *Pardon Us*—in which editing as such is almost nonexistent.

The fateful measuring scene, with Harvey Clark as the tailor.

The Battle of the Century

HAL ROACH—M-G-M, 1927. *Two reels. Directed by Clyde Bruckman. Supervised by Leo McCarey. Story by Hal Roach.*

With Laurel & Hardy, Eugene Pallette, Charlie Hall.

Laurel is a prize fighter, Hardy his opportunistic manager. Since it is apparent that puny little Laurel will never be much of a money-maker in the ring—indeed, he is usually knocked out with the first punch—Hardy listens to a con man's scheme to take out an insurance policy on Laurel. First he borrows money from Laurel to pay for the policy, and then he contrives to have an accident happen. Genuine accidents happen to Laurel all the time, so it stands to reason that a deliberate one is going to be hard to arrange, and it is Hardy who initially takes the falls. Then, a foolproof scheme—a banana peel on the sidewalk. But it is a delivery man (Charles Hall) with a tray of pies who takes the fall, thereby provoking one of the most famous of all Laurel & Hardy slapstick climaxes—the great pie fight.

Henry Miller, whose other writings perhaps make up for his shortcomings as a film historian, once commented that this film came "after thousands of pie-throwing Mack Sennett" comedies. Actually, in the whole history of the movies, there have perhaps been only five all-out pie throwing battles. Chaplin's *Behind the Screen* was the first; this Laurel & Hardy film the second; *Keystone Hotel,* a mediocre two-reel sound short that tried to reconstruct the old zaniness the third; the Three Stooges' *In the Sweet Pie and Pie* the fourth; and the recent *The Great Race* the fifth. The idea that silent slapstick comedy abounded in pie fights is a myth; one finds scattered pies everywhere, hurled with accuracy if not much imagination right through the Sennett era—but they are *single* pies, thrown as punctuation, usually as the only way to start off (or finish) an action or chase sequence. "Custard pie comedy" was, in 1927, a loose phrase used to describe a brand of slapstick considered passé, but the huge-scale and uninhibited fight that Laurel & Hardy perpetrated in this film was more of a climax to a largely undeveloped genre than a reconstruction of it. Like all such Laurel & Hardy sequences, it builds beautifully. There is a reason for the first pie, and the second, and possibly even the third; then reasons turns its back deliberately. Man reverts to the primitive, not because he cannot control himself, but because innately he *wants* to give in to violence—especially when it is a kind of violence that cannot hurt him. Standing on the sidelines of the melee they have started, Laurel & Hardy busily keep the warring factions well supplied with ammunition. "Two?" indicates Laurel with his fingers, and dives into the truck to accommodate his customer. The variety in the ways a pie can be thrown—and the places it can land—are astonishing; and of course it is the innocent bystanders (the patient with his mouth wide open for a tooth extraction, the mailman reaching into the mailbox to grab a handful of unaccountably soggy letters) that suffer the most. A dignified dowager, watching in near-boredom through her lorgnette, receives a pie smack in the face. The opposing factions, quite caught up in their battle to the death, now no longer care what started it or what may end it; they will forget their enmity briefly, however, when some well-meaning neutral steps forward to arbitrate an honorable peace. Then both sides unite to clobber the interloper and send him scurrying amid layers of oozing and dripping whipped cream—an apt commentary perhaps on the frequent sad lot of the diplomat and peacemaker in today's troubled times. Since there is no way to top a spectacular gag sequence like this, the only way to end it is to revert to personalities again—the way it all began. Retreating from the carnage they have caused, which shows no sign of abating, the boys drop their one unused pie to the sidewalk. Striding briskly round the corner comes the magnificent Anita Garvin, chic, elegant, probably out for an evening with the boy friend. She trips, her skirt billows and with a mighty thud she deposits herself right on top of the pie. Unaware of the battle royal raging around the corner, not at all sure of what she has fallen into but full of dread at the dire possibilities, she gets to her feet sheepishly and walks stiff-legged back whence she came, pausing at the corner to shake her leg delicately but futilely.

Until its final third *The Battle of the Century* is rather tame going, but its climactic fight—now justly famous through its inclusion in the Robert Youngson compilation *The Golden Age of Comedy,* for it was strangely overlooked at the time—automatically makes it one of the major Laurel & Hardy works.

Leave 'Em Laughing

HAL ROACH—M-G-M, 1928. *Two reels. Directed by Clyde Bruckman. Supervised by Leo McCarey. Story by Hal Roach.*
   With Laurel & Hardy, Edgar Kennedy.

Laurel is terrified by the rather direct approach of his dentist, who chases his patients around the office, pulls them into his operating room, and wheels out their battered bodies on stretchers. To put his friend's mind at rest and show him how simple it is, Hardy himself sits in the dentist's chair, whereupon the no-time-to-waste dentist returns, sizes up his patient, administers the anesthetic, and has Hardy's teeth out in a trice! Accidentally, the "laughing gas" is turned on, and the boys inhale far too much of it. Laughing hysterically, they amble out into the street and their automobile, where they find that they just cannot take cop Edgar Kennedy's traffic problems seriously. A huge traffic snarl develops, and Kennedy is minus his pants before they finally drive home.

The cure . . .

The outsize toothache . . .

The aftermath

Another of their plotless, two-parter comedies *Leave 'Em Laughing* scores most on the outrageous savagery of the opening sequence. Dentistry has always been a stock prop for Sennett and other film-makers, but only W. C. Fields and Laurel & Hardy have ever been able to make the gags funny enough so that one can forget the pain and unpleasantness involved. There is a priceless moment of facial panto-mime as Hardy comes to in the dentist's chair, realization dawning as his probing tongue gradually discovers and explores the gaps where but a few moments before he had fine healthy teeth, his look of dismay turning to one of resigned suffering when he understands that this is just another misfortune to be chalked up to an association with his friend Mr. Laurel. The second half of the film tends to be rather protracted, although the gags are funny and inventive, and certainly gain from being shot in their entirety in those sunny and hospitable Culver City streets.

The Finishing Touch

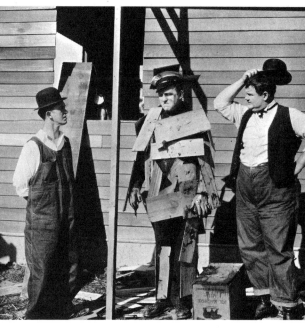

HAL ROACH–M-G-M, 1928. *Two reels. Directed by Clyde Bruckman.*
With Laurel & Hardy, Edgar Kennedy.

Laurel & Hardy, contractors, agree to build a house in one day for an impatient home-owner. Continually harassed by cop Edgar Kennedy and a nurse who begs them to be quiet (they are adjacent to a hospital), they nevertheless finish the job on time. The owner is delighted, and pays up promptly. On cue, a bird settles on the chimney, which collapses, windows and doors following suit. The irate client wants his money back, and the anticipated mutual mayhem begins. A kind of football game develops over the money, Laurel & Hardy passing, the customer trying to intercept. A rock-throwing melee develops and, looking for a particularly heavy rock to fling back, Laurel removes the brick that is acting as a brake to their truck. While they and the home-owner watch in fascinated horror, the truck trundles down the incline towards the house, finishing the demolition job completely.

Considering the promise it offers, *The Finishing Touch* is a slight disappointment. The climactic gags lack the force and "boff" quality that the build-up has led us to expect, and the whole short has a somewhat mechanical flavor to it. Nevertheless, it has energy, and the problems of house construction—Laurel forever removing the board that Hardy is about to step on, slats and glue falling off the roof to encase Edgar Kennedy, the yawning pit of whitewash into which inevitably both Kennedy and the nurse fall—provide every gag with *anticipation* as well as culmination. One of the best running gags is of Hardy continually swallowing mouthfuls of nails (due not to his own carelessness, but to Laurel's unwittingly taking away the steps, boxes, planks, etc. that Hardy confidently expects to be there). The closing scenes also contain a fine sight gag in which the irate customer, Hardy, and Laurel are stretched out in a long line, from far background to immediate foreground. The victimized home-owner heaves a rock at Hardy. Its passage through the air is invisible, but Hardy's hat is almost instantly whisked off; then, after a proportionately overlong delay, Laurel's hat is also plucked from his head as the invisible rock continues on its vengeful way.

From Soup to Nuts

HAL ROACH—M-G-M, 1928. *Two reels. Directed by E. Livingston Kennedy (Edgar Kennedy).*
With Laurel & Hardy, Anita Garvin, Otto Fries, Tiny Sanford.

Laurel & Hardy are waiters of little experience sent by an employment agency to service a dinner at which newly-rich Anita Garvin hopes to impress her friends. She fails.

The first film in which Laurel & Hardy received star billing, *From Soup to Nuts* is actually one of their weaker comedies, being little more than a parade of the traditional slapstick dinner jokes. Laurel spills the soup on the guests; is told to serve

Dignity maintained under trying
conditions by Anita Garvin . . .

. . . and by Tiny Sanford.

The magnificent Miss Garvin eavesdrops.

Laurel flirts with maid Edna Marion.

the salad "undressed" and, in his underwear, belligerently tosses the celery at the diners. A running gag has Laurel constantly tripping Hardy into an outsized cake. Uninspired in content and construction, the film has no genuine climax, and merely stops after two reels. Apart from the always reliable gestures of fastidiousness and embarrassment from Hardy, the really creative comedy in this one comes from Anita Garvin, struggling valiantly with a tiara that is forever falling over her eyes, and barely maintaining dignity and temper as she struggles to capture a cherry that has escaped from her fruit salad, a gag that had been seen earlier in *The Second Hundred Years*. However, in fairness to the film, trite and obvious though it may be, it is good audience material. Scenes from this film included in the compilation *Laurel & Hardy's Laughing Twenties* got bigger, louder, and longer laughs than far subtler material.

You're Darn Tootin'

HAL ROACH–M-G-M, 1928. *Two reels. Directed by Edgar Kennedy. Supervised by Leo McCarey. With Laurel & Hardy, Charles Hall.*

Employed by a municipal orchestra, playing on the bandstand in the park, Laurel & Hardy soon lose their jobs when they run afoul of the conductor, mix up all the sheet music, and generally ruin his performance. Threatened with eviction by their landlady, they seek their fortune as street musicians. Their spectacular lack of success has them tiffing and, in a burst of rage, Laurel throws Hardy's trombone into the street, where it is rolled flat by a truck. Their eye-poking, coat-ripping argument soon develops into a shin-kicking foray which like a raging fever spreads to and embraces all the passers-by. The struggling mass of bruised and cursing humanity soon finds an additional outlet for its hostility in a sudden frenzy of pants-ripping. Strangers are sucked into the great whirlpool of thrashing arms, legs and bodies, disappearing from view, their pants sailing away in mid-air. Even the cop who tries to stop it all, holding tightly to his trousers as he does so, finds them ripped away by the fierce-visaged Laurel, suddenly sobered when he discovers that he has de-pantsed

the long legs of the law. He and Hardy, long since down to their own underwear, make a hasty but graceful retreat, both encased in one oversized pair of pants, tipping their hats politely in farewell as they disappear round a corner.

A variable comedy that gets off to a bad start by relying too much on gags that need sound for punctuation (the precise timing of tapping feet and reactions to single notes of music in the bandstand sequence suggest that originally it may have been planned for music and effects), *You're Darn Tootin'* regains its stride fairly quickly. The boarding house breakfast is a charming sequence with Hardy's fruitless efforts to charm and cajole the landlady; by-play with salt and pepper shakers that Laurel loosens slightly, so that the entire contents are dumped into Hardy's soup, was reworked in one of their talkies,

Hoosegow. The shin-kicking, pants-ripping finale is one of their best and most meticulously constructed sequences of controlled savagery, similar to and in many ways better than the great pie fight.

In passing, it is worth mentioning another Hal Roach comedy of 1928, *A Pair of Tights,* which was presumably intended for Laurel & Hardy, and diverted away from them either because their already full schedule of ten two-reelers for the year could not accommodate it, or because it also contained a shin-kicking episode too close to that of *You're Darn Tootin'*. Edgar Kennedy and Stuart Erwin starred in what were unquestionably roles tailored to Laurel & Hardy, and Charles Hall had some of his best fall-guy footage. It's a pity that Laurel & Hardy didn't make it, for it was both fast and sophisticated, and might well have been one of their major works. Even as it is, it can be considered a minor comedy classic.

Their Purple Moment

HAL ROACH–M-G-M, 1928. *Two reels. Directed by James Parrott. Supervised by Leo McCarey. Camera: George Stevens.*

With Laurel & Hardy, Anita Garvin, Fay Holderness, Leo Willis, Tiny Sanford.

The boys plan a night out bowling, but the wives never leave them enough pocket money for such frivolities. After Mrs. Laurel grabs the latest paycheck, Stan shows Ollie how he has been holding out a little each week, stashing it away in a special hiding place. The ingenious cache is inside a portrait hanging on the wall. Stan proudly shows Ollie how he has cut around the outline of the subject's waistcoat, so that it can be opened to reveal a hidden pocket inside—wherein Stan has been carefully hoarding. Alas, he is unaware that the wives have sneaked back and seen all. As the boys go into the kitchen, the wives remove the money and replace it with worthless cigar coupons, and a few minutes later voice no objections to their menfolk going out for the evening. Chortling over their strategem, the boys retrieve the "money" and head for the bowling alley. However, destiny intervenes in the shape of two young ladies who have been stood up by their boy friends and invite Laurel & Hardy to take their places. Making the most of their night out, the boys agree, heading into an expensive night club, and bidding the cab driver wait, despite an already substantial tab on the meter. For a while all is paradise. The floor show is jazzy and the steaks look delicious. But before they eat, one last reassuring look at that money! The dreadful truth upon him, Laurel cannot touch his meal—nor can he convey his plight to his pal. When Hardy does catch on, he magnanimously passes the check to Stan! By now the suspicious waiter, the irate cab driver and the furious wives, summoned by a gossiping neighbor, all converge on the hapless group, and a free-for-all, with soup as the principal weapon, develops in the kitchen.

A variation on a basic theme that the comedians were to use many times in their career, this is an average subject which depends too much on complicated plotting for there to be enough time for any areas to be explored thoroughly. The climactic bust-up comes too late for it to be built properly, and accordingly it just fizzles out. Nevertheless, the dining sequence, as the pair frantically try to delay paying the bill and to escape during the darkness of the floor show, has some very amusing moments, not least a running gag involving a tray-laden waiter who repeatedly falls over the pair as they crawl under tables in an attempt to escape. The opening sight gag with the portrait is particularly pleasing because, like Keaton's dive through the window into women's clothes in *Sherlock Jr.,* it is a gag that is plausible as well as imaginative, and is done without trickery. Pleasing too is George Stevens' happy plagiarism from *Way Down East*—his photography of the malicious gossip hurrying through the streets with her news matching exactly Bitzer's travel shots of the equivalent gossip in Griffith's 1920 classic. The night club set is unusually elaborate, and thus probably borrowed from another M-G-M production. Despite its flaws, it's an amusing subject. Worth the admission price in itself is one closeup, in the final set-to, of Laurel with thick greasy soup oozing down over his placidly receptive features.

Should Married Men Go Home?

HAL ROACH–M-G-M, 1928. *Two reels. Directed by James Parrott. Supervised by Leo McCarey.*
With Laurel & Hardy, Edgar Kennedy, Viola Ritchard, Edna Marion.

It's a peaceful Sunday morning, and for once, Mr. and Mrs. Hardy are enjoying harmonious relations—so much so that when Mr. Laurel comes calling, they pretend to be out. But Laurel is persistent, and finally Ollie has to let him in. Immediately the peace is shattered (along with a new phonograph) and in disgust Mrs. Hardy, now reverting to her true nature, loses her temper and orders them from the house. The boys head for the golf links, where they soon run into two charming young ladies and quick-tempered Edgar Kennedy. The anticipated clashes don't take long to develop, and the film finishes with the peaceful Sunday air disrupted by a full-scale mud-slinging fight.

One of the best of the "forgotten" Laurel & Hardy films, *Should Married Men Go Home?* admittedly overlaps with several of their other films but is no

Laurel helpfully points out to Edgar Kennedy that he is wearing some golf links turf, not a toupee.

less funny because of it. The opening sequence, of the Hardys pretending to be out, worked rather better the second time (in *Come Clean*), where it had the benefit of dialogue. However, the original has a beautiful gag not used in the later version. As the boys leave the house in disgrace, Laurel, nattily attired in the latest golfing togs, places his hand on the neat white picket fence surrounding the house and takes an agile, Fairbanksian leap over it. Hardy, noting that his wife is watching, and determined to both impress her and put her in her place, decides to do likewise. Firmly, he places *his* pudgy hand on the fence too—but his leap doesn't quite come off, and the fence collapses beneath his weight! When the pair pick up the two girls at the golf course, there is the problem of buying them refreshments with not enough money to go around. Hardy, unwilling of course to admit that he is anything but the soul of generosity and affluence, sees a way out. He will ask Laurel what *he* wants, and Laurel will refuse. Laurel doesn't quite understand, and after his first refusal, gives in to Hardy's repeated request to order something. This sequence, a trifle protracted, again worked rather better when it was redone with dialogue in

Men o'War. Out on the links, the altercations with Edgar Kennedy include a memorable scene where his patently phony wig falls from his bald dome. Embarrassed, he tries to retrieve it, and in his haste to be a good fellow, Laurel hands him a divot from the course, with a toupee-like area of turf attached. Poor Kennedy, close-cropped grass on his head, little daisies seemingly growing from his scalp, goes into his customary slow-burn. When Laurel insists that he play his ball from where it came to rest, as the rules state, Kennedy finds himself trapped in a mud hollow. Frantic swings with his club sends great chunks of mud soaring in all directions with unerring accuracy, and the besplattered golfers converge on all sides for a muddy equivalent of the great pie fight.

Incidentally, Viola Ritchard, one of the two leading ladies, is a quite undeservedly forgotten comedienne. She appeared in many of the Laurel & Hardy and Charlie Chase comedies for Roach, both at Pathé and M-G-M. Attractive, pert, and vivacious, with a fine sense of comedy timing, she should have gone much further than she did—and probably would have, had not a striking resemblance to Clara Bow, then at her peak, held her back from important roles.

66

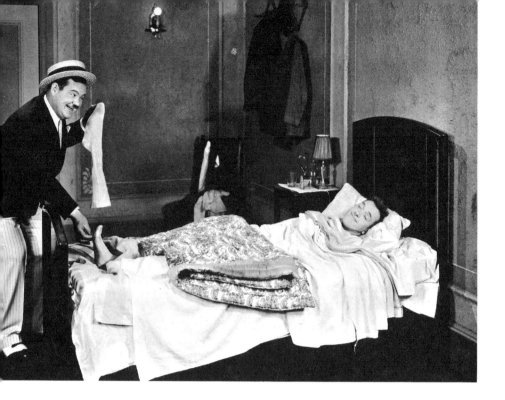

Early to Bed

HAL ROACH—M-G-M, 1928. *Two reels. Directed by Emmett Flynn.*
  With Laurel & Hardy.

Hardy suddenly inherits a fortune, installs himself in a mansion with costly new furniture and décor, and puts his erstwhile buddy Stan to work as his butler. Stan is conscientious, but Ollie, revelling in his new-found power and affluence, takes delight in torment-ing his pal, pouring ice-water on him while he sleeps, and so on. Stan finally rebels, and threatens to resign. Inadvertently, a piece of Hardy's expensive new fur-niture is damaged and, seeing Hardy's horror, Laurel realizes *his* power. Systematically he goes on a ram-page of destruction, Hardy trying desperately to save the huge vases and other bric-a-brac that are crashing around him.

Although a lesser Laurel & Hardy, *Early to Bed* contains good gags, amusing titles, and an interesting variation on the usual relationship between them. Laurel's retaliatory bursts of vengeance were infre-quent, but fairly evenly spaced in about one picture in eight, so that to those who saw all their films the cumulative effect was even funnier, such sequences

acting as a kind of steam-valve in the overall saga of Laurel & Hardy. *Early to Bed,* however, is climaxed by a magnificent sight gag which, curiously, they never repeated—perhaps because they themselves had borrowed it from an earlier Roach comedy with Mabel Normand. Mabel's film barely scratched at the surface of the gag's possibilities, however, while Laurel & Hardy milked it for all it was worth. During a climactic chase sequence, Hardy takes refuge in the garden. Dominating the set is an elaborate decorative fountain, its base encircled by a number of identical little stone cherub heads, from the mouths of which pour forth steady streams of water. Coincidentally, these little heads are dead ringers for Oliver Hardy! To escape detection, Hardy submerges himself in the water, removes one of the stone heads, and rests his own head on its pedestal. He even contrives to eject a constant though none too steady flow of water from his mouth. The head, somehow a little different from all the others, attracts Laurel's attention. Under his close scrutiny, Hardy remains immobile, eyes starring glassily ahead, water continuing to pour forth from this human fountain. But, inevitably, Hardy's well runs dry. With all the other cherub heads in perfect working order, Laurel deduces that this one has developed a mechanical defect. Perhaps if he knocks it a few times the clogged mechanism will free itself. Further verbal elaboration on this gag is surely unnecessary; it's one of the most captivating routines they ever did, and must have delighted Buñuel, Dali, and the other surrealists who were just beginning to delve into film at that time.

Two Tars

HAL ROACH—M-G-M, 1928. *Two reels. Directed by James Parrott. Camera: George Stevens.*
  With Laurel & Hardy, Edgar Kennedy, Charles Hall.

Laurel & Hardy, sailors on leave, rent a car and pick up two girls for a drive in the country. An initial altercation with drug store owner Charles Hall—in which the two tars are egged on by the girls, impatient to get going and have fun—is followed by an even more spectacular set-to when they hit the open road. Road repairs have caused a massive traffic tie-up, and with the long delay having already caused tempers to reach the breaking point, Hardy's intervention is not welcomed. Like a brush fire, antagonisms race, leap and roar into life, so that before long the waiting motorists are at each other's throats. Finally, the all-but-destroyed cars limp off in a freakish parade, some of them in hot pursuit of the two tars, who lead them into a railroad tunnel just before a locomotive enters, thus completing the destruction of a peaceful Sunday afternoon.

Originally titled *Two Tough Tars* and running for three reels, the title and running time were both whittled down until, in its two-reel form, it became both one of the most elaborate short comedies ever made and certainly one of Laurel & Hardy's most famous. The introductory "battle" with Charles Hall seems a trifle forced, but perhaps only because we

The beginning of a perfect day.

Early hostilities.

know what lies ahead, and are eager to be at it. As always, the full-scale war develops out of the smallest incidents of belligerence—oil is accidentally squirted in a motorist's face, and the delighted squeals of the two girls are not altogether conducive to patient understanding of the situation; cars are bumped unin-

tentionally; the carefully arranged luggage, tied on top and sides of a rickety car, is pulled into the dust. But once admonitions prove to be insufficient, the kid gloves are removed and orderly but unlimited destruction takes over—ranging from a pile of mud, carefully collected and moulded into shape in front of

69

the victim's unwavering eyes, dumped on his head, squashed flat and held in place by his bowler hat, to the ultimate demolition of all the cars in sight by yanking off hoods, doors and wheels. Despite the sheer size of the comedy—and obviously a hundred or more cars and trucks were lined up on that sunny California highway—it is as usual the gentler bits of individual humor that register best. Especially memorable is Laurel's pained and indignant expression (as though the act was not in accordance with the rules) when a hurled tomato hits him on the back of the neck, and slowly and juicily slips down the back of his sailor uniform; and another moment when an unfortunate motorist has aroused their particular ire, and, with a knowing affirmative nod at each other, they hoist up their belts in the time-honored nautical fashion, march over to the car, flank it, and without a word being spoken, pull off the front wheels simultaneously so that the poor crippled auto lurches down on its gas tank like a bewildered bulldogged steer.

Next to *Big Business,* which is better only because it is simpler, *Two Tars* is about the funniest and most representative of all Laurel & Hardy silents.

Edgar Kennedy (rear car), before and after.

70

Habeas Corpus

HAL ROACH—M-G-M, 1928. *Two reels. Directed by Leo McCarey.*
With Laurel & Hardy, Richard Carle.

Genially mad scientist Richard Carle hires the boys to steal bodies from a cemetery for his experiments.

Very funny, *Habeas Corpus* is rather more a matter of traditional slapstick routines than was usual with Laurel & Hardy. There's the old gag of climb- ing a signpost at night to read directions, only to find that it is a "wet paint" sign; another standard routine in which an apparent corpse in the sack that Hardy is carrying is actually very much alive, his hands and feet emerging through holes in the sack so that he is walking on all fours; Laurel & Hardy scaling a wall only to have it collapse beneath them. Curiously, although Leo McCarey supervised many of the best Laurel & Hardy comedies, the three that he directed personally were neither typical McCarey nor typical Laurel & Hardy.

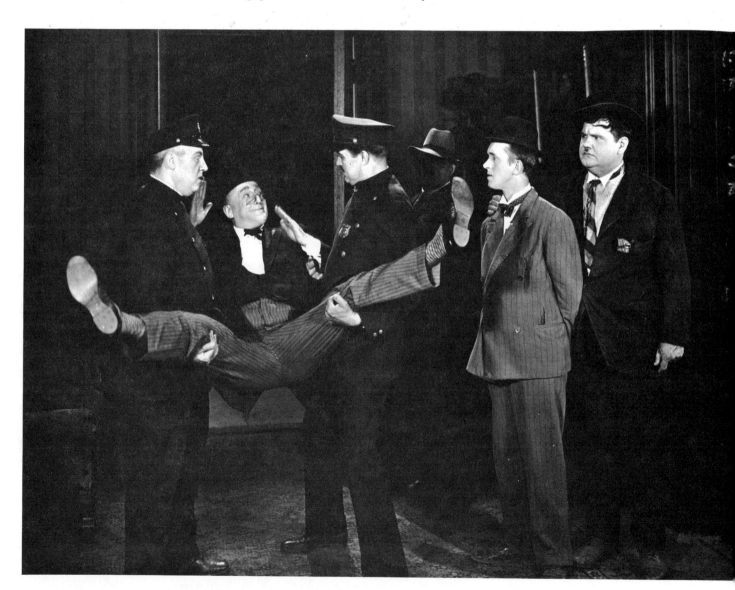

We Faw Down

HAL ROACH—M-G-M, 1928. *Two reels. Also known as* WE SLIP UP. *Directed by Leo McCarey. With Laurel & Hardy.*

Cheating (harmlessly) on their wives, the boys go out for a poker game, although officially they have gone to a show. When the wives hear that the theatre has suddenly burned down, they are remorse-stricken. But by this time, the two husbands have gotten soaked in a mud puddle and have been taken in by two flirtatious girls with a convenient apartment. Dis-

Sudden realization that their alibi of being at the theatre will now take some explaining.

The precipitate arrival of a jealous boy friend.

covering them, the wives quickly change from mourners back to their normal vengeful selves.

The basic idea of *We Faw Down,* itself borrowed from an old Mack Sennett-Mack Swain comedy called *Ambrose's First Falsehood,* was later reworked by Laurel & Hardy into their most sophisticated feature, *Sons of the Desert. We Faw Down* is, on the whole, rather draggy and pedestrian, though it has isolated gags that are among their best. Particularly amusing are the two flirts' attempts to inject some life into their two pickups. One of them, mildly drunk, finds that poking Laurel's Adam's apple produces an immediate reflex-action with his tongue.

The best gag of all however, is the climactic one. The wives, armed with shotguns, arrive just as Laurel & Hardy, minus their trousers, are beating an undignified retreat from the rear window of an apartment house. Like hunters taking aim at birds on the rise, the wives let go with the shotguns—and instantly each window of the apartment house ejects its quota of trouserless cheating husbands, some clambering unceremoniously from ground floor windows, others leaping desperately from higher windows or seeking the fire escape. It's a brilliant and untoppable climactic gag, and one that the comedians were to repeat, though less successfully, in their sound feature *Blockheads.*

Liberty

HAL ROACH—M-G-M, 1929. *Two reels, released in silent and limited sound versions. Directed by Leo McCarey.*

With Laurel & Hardy, James Finlayson, Tom Kennedy, Jean Harlow.

Escaping from prison, Laurel & Hardy are picked up by confederates and put on civilian clothes in the cramped quarters of a car. Out on the street, they find that each is wearing the other's pants, and at-

tempts to change clothes with each other finally lead to their being stranded on the high girders of a skyscraper. Ultimately they do manage to change pants, avoid a suspicious cop, and escape to presumably permanent freedom.

An unusual and skilful excursion into the building-climbing comedy-thrill domain of Harold Lloyd, *Liberty* (for years known as *Criminals at Large,* because of bootlegged prints bearing that title) has some of Laurel & Hardy's funniest material. Pursued by cops

at the beginning, they slip out of their escape car as it rounds a bend, and instantly strike a pose of nonchalant and approving inspection of a stationary auto, as the law races by. The pants-changing routine affords them some of their choicest and most risqué comedy of embarrassment, for they are forever being discovered behind walls or packing crates, furtively lowering their pants. A woman looks out of her apartment window at the scene below and screams. A cop sees and pursues, only to lose them. He stands bemused in front of a pile of packing cases—which then descend below street level on an elevator, to reveal the boys behind it, fussily trying to expedite the exchange of the too-tight and too-loose pants. Discovered, Stan beams broadly, innocently unaware

of any dubious interpretations that could be placed on their actions. Hardy, all *too* aware of the obvious reactions, twiddles his tie, shifts his feet sheepishly, offers a coy smile and hopes that no questions will be asked.

At one point the pants gag seems to have been dropped in favor of a new story tangent. A cab stands waiting at a corner, and a young man and his girl friend (Jean Harlow) step into it. But before they are fully inside, the girl recoils in horror and steps back. Out steps Oliver, hastily buttoning his pants, followed by Stan. Inspecting the inside of the cab carefully this time, Miss Harlow and her escort deem it reasonably safe, and get in. The pants gag is developed still further when, during one of the

74

thwarted exchanges, a lively lobster drops himself into Laurel's trousers. He nips Laurel at such regular intervals that Laurel retraces his steps to see what there is about *that* particular stretch of sidewalk that so affects him! James Finlayson, store proprietor, comes on to the street with a large pile of phonograph records, pop-eyed and scowling at the audience in general, defying anyone to risk defiling such an obvious slapstick prop. His immediate encounter with Laurel not only demolishes his entire stock within seconds, but convinces him that he is threatened by a maniac! Another attempt to change the troublesome pants—this time on a construction unit—where again they are discovered, by rugged he-man laborers who glare at them in contempt!

Liberty's last half, enacted high up on the skeleton of the skyscraper, sees the pants finally changed despite the opposition of loose girders, falling sandbags and a still-rampaging lobster. It is flawlessly done, technically quite up to the Harold Lloyd standards, though rather alien to Laurel & Hardy's usual style. However, the confrontation by a situation of real danger permits the exploitation of Laurel-Hardy character traits often untouched. Hardy, nervous, nevertheless steels himself to go to the aid of Laurel, hanging from a girder. But as he hauls him to safety, his own position duplicates Laurel's; hastily he shoves his friend back into jeopardy, re-establishes his own security, and then on his knees offers up a brief prayer in lieu of risking his life again!

In their few prison films, Laurel & Hardy more than paid for their (usually unspecified) crimes, and escapes were transient things at best. Here, however, they go scot-free, after first crushing their cop-pursuer in an elevator and transforming him from a vigorous six-footer to a pint-sized midget.

Wrong Again

HAL ROACH—M-G-M, 1929. *Two reels, released in silent and limited sound versions. Directed by Leo McCarey.*

With Laurel & Hardy, Anders Randolph, Josephine Crowell, Fred Kelsey.

Stable-hands Laurel & Hardy hear of the huge reward offered for the return of "Blue Boy." It is the famous painting that has been stolen, but they assume it is a horse of the same name, kept in their stables. Appropriating the horse, they take it to the millionaire-owner of the painting, who, upstairs, calls down to them to bring "Blue Boy" in and place it on the piano. The misunderstanding is played to the hilt until the real "Blue Boy" painting arrives—and of course is immediately destroyed!

An off-beat comedy that can only be seen at a disadvantage now in that it was made as both a silent and limited sound release, and undoubtedly paced for sound. Today only the silent version survives, and at times seems awkward and unsure of itself. Nevertheless, it has some very funny moments. One of the best running gags involves Laurel's breaking (into three parts) of a nude Greek statue, which he re-assembles with the trunk portion reversed. Hardy tells him that millionaires are all eccentric and do everything "twisted around," and Laurel's attempts to equate this information with the peculiar anatomical structure of the statue gives him full scope for that healthily vulgar pantomime that he could do so well. Most of the action, however, is physical slapstick—though of a measured, well-controlled nature—dealing primarily with attempts to control the horse within the house, and to get it safely atop the piano. At one point the piano collapses, a leg breaking off, and Laurel attempts to remedy it while Hardy supports piano (and horse) from a hands and knees position. Laurel's below-screen fumblings are revealed when the camera pulls back to show Hardy's tortured body still in position, the piano leg now resting under his chin supporting *him.* There is a semi-surrealistic quality to many of the sight gags in *Wrong Again,* and one would like to think that Laurel & Hardy were kidding the Dali-Buñuel *Un Chien Andalou* (with its donkeys on a piano) which they could well have seen (it was a 1928 production) before making this film.

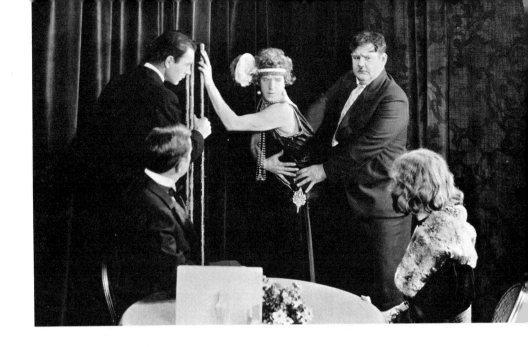

That's My Wife

HAL ROACH–M-G-M, 1929. *Two reels. Directed by Lloyd French.*
  With Laurel & Hardy, Dorothy Christie.

Just after Hardy's wife has left him in disgust, his rich uncle arrives, almost immediately reminding him that he will be left everything–providing of course he remains happily married. Fortuitously, Stanley is upstairs, and is persuaded to masquerade as Mrs. Hardy. To entertain Uncle, Mr. and "Mrs." Hardy take him to a night club–where, inevitably, the deception is finally discovered and once more Hardy's little world collapses around his ears.

Comparatively little known, this is perhaps the funniest and best of the many films in which Laurel masquerades as a woman. The single theme is handled with infinite variety throughout, starting with Mrs. Hardy's determined bag-packing and her pronouncement that she is leaving. "Why?" asks Hardy plaintively, and in mute but eloquent answer Mrs. Hardy points to Mr. Laurel, an innocent onlooker at the marriage he has cut in twain merely by his presence. Laurel, with exercising dumb-bells for a bosom, makes a most fetching dame, and the night club sequence, which is the larger part of the film, keeps on the move with a number of running gags which are developed in parallel rather than consecutive sequence. One of these, originating in *Their Purple Moment,* is of the tripping of a waiter, a gag handled with astonishing variety. Another, a variation on the pants gag in *Liberty,* has a pendant accidentally dropped down the back of Laurel's dress. Hardy's efforts to retrieve it invariably result in his being discovered–behind a curtain or in a phone booth–with his hand reaching down the back of his wife's dress. This gag, not over-prolonged, reaches its climax when the m.c. of the night club announces the big entertainment event of the evening, Norman and Lucille performing "The Dance of Love." The curtains are pulled back dramatically, and there on all fours are Mr. and "Mrs." Hardy! Another running gag which provides the film with an unanticipated climax is of a drunk's flirtations with Laurel. Finally, unable to bear it any longer, Laurel permits himself the unladylike luxury of flinging a bowl of soup into the drunk's face. Quite calmly, the drunk calls for his check–and "a bowl of soup to go." Apparently he has been disposed of. The plot rolls along its merry way to the ultimate unmasking of Stan, uncle's shock, and his inevitable announcement that Hardy can not expect one penny of his estate. Out in the street, Hardy is at his most crestfallen, and ticks off his misfortunes to Laurel. "I've lost my wife. I've lost my uncle's inheritance. I've been disgraced. What *more* can happen to me?" In answer, a great bowl of greasy soup is hurled out of nowhere, and the film closes on a sticky closeup of the unfortunate Oliver Hardy.

Big Business

HAL ROACH—M-G-M, 1929. *Two reels. Directed by James Horne.*

With Laurel & Hardy, James Finlayson, Tiny Sanford.

Laurel & Hardy are Christmas tree salesmen whose salesmanship in sunny California in mid-July is not producing very concrete results, even when they follow up a turndown by trying to get advance orders for the following year. Taking refusals in their stride, they determine to make of James Finlayson a "test case" to prove their salesmanship when his obstinacy becomes a little too firm. Soon Christmas trees are forgotten, and in the battle royal that follows, their business—and his home—are totally wrecked.

The apotheosis of all Laurel & Hardy films, and a subject that one could not imprudently label the funniest two reels on film, *Big Business* is one of *the* comedy classics from any star, any country and any period. Even non-Laurel & Hardy devotees are automatically caught up in the maelstrom of fury which, in its precise mounting excitement, attention to detail, meticulous editing, and no-pause-for-breath action, is to the comedy film what *The Birth of a Nation* is to the historical spectacle. Even the preliminary skirmishing, which *has* to be on the intimate, personal level, is hilarious. Finlayson takes, examines, and winks approvingly at Hardy's watch, assuring him that it is in perfect working order, and then in one wild gesture smashes it to the sidewalk, and tramples on it. Hardy slices slivers of woodwork from Finlayson's front door, but has his shirt clipped in retaliation. Laurel pries the street-numbers from Finlayson's front door, and when Finlayson tries to call the police, the phone wire is cut in half in his very hands. Time for honorable negotiation and settlement now being past, the implements of war are brought forth— gardening hose, shears, spades, bricks. As Laurel & Hardy break a window, so Finlayson breaks the windshield of their car, via a brick hurled at two paces. Soon even the back-and-forth, eye-for-an-eye warfare is discarded; Laurel & Hardy dedicate themselves to the full-scale destruction of Finlayson's house, while he launches an offensive against their car. When Laurel & Hardy have finished with the house, there is still the garden, and when trees have been toppled and shrubbery yanked out by the roots, the boys fall back on the smooth lawn, which is soon filled with potholes. Their car offers Finlayson less potential; after he has ripped off the gas tank and broken doors and wheels, he does battle with their supply of Christmas trees. Then—a match applied to the leaking gas tank, and everything explodes in a

mass of burned rubble. Still Finlayson seeks to add injury to insult. With a hammer, he skips gaily and triumphantly over the wreckage, seeking out any piece of it that still has a shape, and hammering it flat.

This incredible spectacle has of course been watched by a growing number of curious but passive neighbors and passers-by, including policeman Tiny Sanford, whose expression indicates contempt for such childish goings-on, but whose respect for the due process of law impells him to remain silent, making copious notes, until he is galvanized into personal intervention by a spade landing on his foot, when Mr. Hardy, adopting the stance of a baseball player, hits and demolishes all the vases and other bric-a-brac that Laurel is throwing from inside the house. The presence of the law brings Hardy up short; Laurel, as yet blissfully unaware of it, trundles a piano onto the lawn, reduces it to kindling with a

few deft strokes of an axe, and then, when he too becomes cognizant of the forces of law and order, strives somewhat fruitlessly to reassemble the shattered keyboard. The opposing forces are brought together in a truce and survey the battlefield. Finlayson's home has been ruined, but presumably can be repaired. Laurel & Hardy's loss is more serious. Their business, their stock, their transportation, one suspects also their home—all totally gone. The erstwhile enemies dissolve into sentimentality and forgive each other; to show his good faith, Hardy presents Finlayson with a cigar. But alone, their faces take on a conspiratorial air and they break into chuckles; their remorse but a sham, they are honest enough to admit having enjoyed the fracas to the full. The policeman sees their mirth, however, and takes after them—their flight punctuated by an explosion from Finlayson's cigar, the last gesture that establishes them as the victors in the titanic struggle.

Double Whoopee

Moments before Jean Harlow's dress
is caught in the taxi door . . .

. . . and moments after!

HAL ROACH—M-G-M, 1929. *Two reels. Directed by Lewis Foster. Story by Leo McCarey. With Laurel & Hardy, Jean Harlow, Charles Hall.*

Laurel & Hardy make their appearance at a swank New York hotel just as it is all agog over the impending arrival of a European prince. In the confusion, Stan and Ollie are assumed to be the visiting royalty, and given the red carpet treatment—only for the carpet to be yanked vigorously from under them when the real prince arrives. Revealed as humble doormen—and not very good ones at that, for the agency sends along an apology with their letter of introduction—the boys set to work with a maximum of good intentions and a minimum of ability. Before too long they have antagonized most of the hotel's guests, earned the enmity of local cop and cab driver alike, and reduced the poor prince to a state of almost declaring war. Taking the hint that their services are no longer required, they leave with as much aplomb and dignity as they arrived.

Double Whoopee is sufficiently different from the general run of Laurel & Hardy comedies that one would *like* it to be among their best, and while it never does quite live up to its potential, it does manage to remain one of their better silent comedies. Deliberate repetition is again the foundation of its many gags, the most elaborate of which is a play on princely vanity. The Prince—a cigar-smoking, monocled satire of the von Stroheim of *Foolish Wives*—frequently is about to enter an elevator, frequently digresses for a moment to deliver a pompous statement to his audience, and—as frequently—turns to plunge into a now-empty elevator shaft, Laurel or Hardy having taken the elevator elsewhere in the meantime. Each fall is followed by Laurel & Hardy stepping briskly from the elevator, serenely unaware of the international havoc they have caused, and marching off to their duties while the outraged prince arises from the depths of the dirty shaft, spluttering with rage, his dignity injured and his spotless white uniform covered with oil and grease. The gag is repeated with variations several times, gaining from audience foreknowledge of what is to happen, and it also serves as the wrap-up gag when Laurel & Hardy, their bags packed, saunter jauntily from the elevator and out into the night, still unaware that their latest and final descent has once more plunged the prince to a muddy fate!

Other gags are repeated throughout the film, but most of them are unique to this comedy, and only one was ever used again—a long "signing the hotel register" routine in which Hardy goes to extreme lengths to observe the necessary etiquette of having Laurel remove his hat while signing; and Laurel's long, labored study of the register, his positioning of

Laurel helps a customer on with his coat — and off with his shirt.

himself to sign, his resenting of Hardy's looking over his shoulder, the spilling of a bottle of ink over the register, and ultimately the signing itself—a very careful "X". This routine was to be re-used almost verbatim in the talkie *Any Old Port,* where it became even funnier due to being set in a sleazy flea-bag of a hotel, with roughneck proprietor Walter Long watching the whole rigamarole in impatient wonder.

For the rest, *Double Whoopee* is typically fast and violent, with the inevitable eye-pokings and a glorious moment wherein a suddenly enraged Laurel, stripped to his underwear and mad at the world, takes on all comers, friend and foe alike, ripping the shirt off one embarrassed hotel guest, then following through by yanking a large plaster-pad off his chest in one painful rip, and solicitously stuffing back into

the man's miraculously intact vest some of the chest-hair that became detached in the operation!

Because of the basic set-up—Hardy, a resplendently uniformed doorman a la Emil Jannings in *The Last Laugh,* overly-ingratiating to guests, trying to instill dignity for their new profession into Laurel, and at the same time keep him in his place as his own subordinate—there is an even wider field than usual for Hardy's pantomime of face and body, and he—and the gloriously lampooned Stroheim—tend to rather dominate Stan on this occasion. Jean Harlow, looking sexy and attractive as a young lady whose skirt is ripped away accidentally by the mortified Hardy, is actually no more than a comedy prop, despite the "dressing" she gives to her short but memorable sequence.

The Prince's honor — and his uniform — stained in the elevator shaft.

The dignified beginning of a train ride.

Berth Marks

HAL ROACH—M-G-M, 1929. *Two reels, released in both silent and sound versions. Directed by Lewis Foster. Story by Leo McCarey.*

With Laurel & Hardy, Charles Hall, and Paulette Goddard as an extra.

Laurel & Hardy are itinerant musicians, trying to get from one unimportant engagement in a hick town to an even smaller engagement in another hick town.

After a sleepless night in an upper berth, they arrive sooner than they expect, beat a hasty exit from the train in their underclothes, and realize too late that they have left their instruments on board.

One of the few really poor comedies that the team made, this is a misfire all down the line. The blame cannot be laid entirely on its paucity of plot, since single situations often stood them in good stead, and a similarly simple exercise in frustration, *Below Zero,*

An altercation en route, with Laurel & Hardy, the cause of it all, calmly aloof.

83

had a great deal of merit. Possibly the main problem with *Berth Marks* is that it is essentially *visual* pantomime, for more than half of the film consists of them trying to undress, get comfortable and go to sleep in a cramped upper berth on the train, and such a precise and limited comedy situation requires the expert timing which they just could not give it when the film was being shot for both sound and silent release. Wholly silent or wholly sound, it might have worked; the compromise between the two was merely tiresome. Likewise, a shirt-ripping scene—deriving of course from the pants-ripping of *You're Darn Tootin'*—fell between the two schools and failed. The only genuinely amusing sequence in the entire film was at the very beginning (though this too would have failed in a completely silent version) where Laurel & Hardy arrive at the railroad station, and attempt to make sense of the rapid-fire gibberish of unheard-of small town names that the conductor rattles off at top speed, and then repeats under Hardy's embarrased questioning. There is some genuine wit in this episode, with dialogue used sparingly but to good effect. Unfortunately, it is quite nullified by the dull two reels that follow. The sleeping-berth sequence was reworked into one of their last features, *The Big Noise,* where it worked rather better but was still too protracted.

The less dignified end of the ride.

A misunderstanding: It's her *gloves* the lady has lost!

Men O'War

HAL ROACH–M-G-M, 1929. *Two reels, released in both silent and sound versions. Directed by Lewis Foster. Story by Leo McCarey.*

With Laurel & Hardy, James Finlayson, Charlie Hall.

Two sailors on leave and out for a good time pick up a couple of girls in the park. They want to impress the girls as big spenders and give them a good time—which is a little difficult on a total budget of fifteen cents. Hardy works out a foolproof scheme, which fails, leaving Laurel to face an irate soda jerk with a bill he can't pay. Trusting to providence, Laurel invests the only money he has in a slot-machine—and wins! With their new wealth they take the girls boating, but their seamanship isn't up to the intricacies of a rowboat. Minor collisions and insults hurled across the waters develop into more vigorous differences of opinion, and the boys are soon literally scuttled.

A tremendous improvement on *Berth Marks, Men O'War*—which is obviously inspired by, but does not copy, *Two Tars*—is still a trifle uncertain and over-emphatic in its pacing, but manages to be very funny throughout although it undoubtedly works better as a talkie. One of the very few Laurel & Hardy comedies shot entirely on location with no studio work at all, *Men O'War* takes place in one of those cheerful, sunny, and photogenic Hollywood parks where the strollers seem so blasé about slapstick comedy-makers that they never gawk at the goings-on. Until the final episode, dialogue carries the story. Hardy finds a pair of white panties in the park. Simultaneously we learn that one of the girls has lost a pair of white gloves. Inevitably, Hardy and flapper meet, Hardy too embarrassed to mention the garment by name—other than to indicate that he has found what she is looking for—and the girl, enjoying the mild flirtation anyway, not thinking it necessary. "I bet you miss them!" suggests Hardy, with an embarrassed turning away of his face, yet a roguish twinkle in his eye

Nautical cunning – a plan to buy sodas for four with only fifteen cents.

indicating satisfaction with his own boldness. "Well, you can *just* imagine," replies the young lady; "they were so easy to slip off, and I washed them with gasoline just this morning!" So it goes, each double-entendre causing Hardy to stare dubiously at the audience, as if hoping for some kind of guidance, or at least an explanation as to what kind of girl he has to cope with! Finally a cop returns the missing gloves, Hardy hastily ditches the panties, and they're off to a good time at James Finlayson's ice cream parlor. Because of the limited funds, Laurel is to refuse when asked what he wants to drink—but of course he cannot sustain that thought past the first refusal.

Pressured by the girls to be a sport, he gives in and orders a chocolate soda. "Pardon me, just a minute" pleads Hardy, taking Laurel off to the side to go through it all again. "Can't you *grasp* the situation?" he asks exasperatedly. Laurel catches on—apparently —but the situation repeats itself several times, to Finlayson's increasing lack of patience. Finally Laurel agrees to refuse, and settles for half of Hardy's soda. When the soda arrives, he drains it to the last drop. "My half was on the bottom" is his anticipated answer. This whole routine, paced better in the silent *Should Married Men Go Home?*, nevertheless works more effectively in this wholly sound treatment, de-

The end of a typical Laurel & Hardy day; Charles Hall at extreme left, James Finlayson at extreme right.

spite the occasional distractions of whirring camera noises.

The final sequence of mayhem aboard the row-boats again suffers from the uncertainty of pacing prevalent in so many early talkies. Shots generally tend to go on too long, and funny though he is, there are certainly too many cutaways to James Finlayson mugging and reacting. Nevertheless, the conception is good, and the sequence builds: minor insult leading to major insult, hurled pillow to striking fist, one collision to many. Soon most of the boaters on the lake have been grounded, stalled or sunk, and to a man they come swimming and splashing to the Laurel & Hardy boat, where they all clamber aboard to continue the fight until the sheer weight of numbers causes boat, girls, sailors and battling boaters to sink majestically beneath the waters.

A Perfect Day

HAL ROACH—M-G-M, 1929. *Two reels, released in both silent and sound versions. Directed by James Parrott. Story by Leo McCarey.*
With Laurel & Hardy, Edgar Kennedy.

Laurel & Hardy and the wives decide to spend a day in the country picnicking. Gout-ridden uncle Edgar Kennedy would prefer to stay home and suffer peacefully, but is finally persuaded to come along. However, the best laid schemes exercise their usual prerogative, and the delays are endless. When finally all is ready, their automobile calmly sinks into a mud hole, ending the perfect day almost before it has begun.

Another essay in prolonged frustration, *A Perfect Day* is never quite equal in its execution to its concept, perhaps because such an unrelieved succession of frustrations can prove irksome to an audience too. The sandwiches are carefully prepared, and then dumped all over the floor, thanks to Mr. Laurel's carelessness—only to be somewhat unhygenically retrieved and repacked. Stan and Ollie soon lose their tempers with each other, only to be admonished by the wives not to fight on the Sabbath. Kennedy's gout-ridden foot is continually being trodden on—or crushed beneath the wheel of the automobile. Enthusiastic goodbyes to the neighbors are followed by much spluttering and choking from the reluctant auto, which refuses to start. One of the less friendly

The perfect day begins with the sandwiches being spilled on the floor.

neighbors gets involved in one of Laurel & Hardy's little private wars, but this is terminated before too much damage can be done by the untimely arrival of the local minister on his way to church. The wives grow steadily less helpful and more irritating with their backseat comments, and in a rare moment of retaliation, Ollie turns on Mrs. H. and silences her with a long stare of barely contained fury. Finally, thanks to an angry kick, the car does start—and heads right into one of those six-foot-deep mud puddles with which Laurel & Hardy's world was so generously supplied. Once more, the use of sound is often quite creative, and individual sequences are fine, but the subject as a whole lacks finesse.

They Go Boom

HAL ROACH—M-G-M, 1929. *Two reels. Directed by James Parrott. Story by Leo McCarey. With Laurel & Hardy.*

Ollie has a severe head cold, and Stan consents to sweat it out with him. Waiting on him hand and foot, Laurel's well-meant efforts just don't seem to work out, and their small rented room is all but demolished by Stan's tender ministrations.

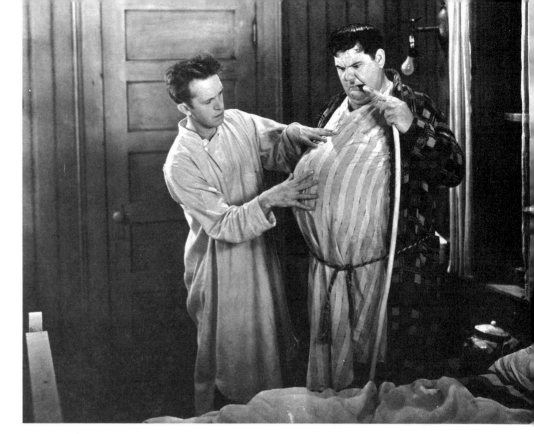

Another of Laurel & Hardy's gags of physical distortion.

Like *Berth Marks* and *A Perfect Day, They Go Boom* is another meticulous exploitation of a single situation—something that they apparently felt was a good formula for early sound films that had also been released in silent form. *Berth Marks* was easily the weakest film to emerge from this brand of thinking, but *They Go Boom* was better, albeit inferior to *Men O'War* and *A Perfect Day,* and on the whole, one of their weaker subjects.

The familiar triangle: Hardy is coy and apologetic, Laurel blissfully innocent, landlord Charlie Hall at the end of his rope.

89

Bacon Grabbers

HAL ROACH—M-G-M, 1929. *Two reels, released in both silent and limited sound versions. Directed by Lewis Foster. Story by Leo McCarey. Camera: George Stevens.*

With Laurel & Hardy, Edgar Kennedy, Charles Hall, Jean Harlow.

Laurel & Hardy are process servers, ordered to serve a summons on Edgar Kennedy and retrieve a radio he has not paid for.

Originally released with a musical score and special sound effects, recorded on disc by the Victor Talking Machine Company, *Bacon Grabbers,* which of course was also released in silent form, occasionally seems a trifle off in its pacing because of this deliberate utilization of specific moments of sound However, it contained no dialogue at all, and so is essentially a purely visual comedy and thus better constructed than the few in-between subjects that had preceded it. Like *Big Business,* which it resembles in structure, it takes a single simple situation and manages to both milk every gag and at the same time build comic tension steadily until it reaches near-frenzy. The film is divided into two definite halves: their attempts to serve Edgar Kennedy with the summons for the radio, and when they finally succeed in this, their attempts to seize the radio itself when Kennedy adopts a "try and get it!" attitude. The first half is probably the better, the sequences of Laurel & Hardy pursuing Kennedy in and around his house, avoiding a ferocious dog, losing the paper at the crucial moment, handing him a ham sandwich instead of the summons, achieving a remarkable perfection of timing and a ballet-like grace which the second half, with more standard and faster slapstick, does not duplicate.

On the whole, it is one of the better films from their rather variable 1929 offerings. Jean Harlow is seen briefly in the closing scenes as Edgar Kennedy's wife.

Angora Love

HAL ROACH—M-G-M, 1929. *Two reels. Directed by Lewis Foster. Story by Leo McCarey. Camera: George Stevens.*

With Laurel & Hardy, Edgar Kennedy.

A stray goat affectionately attaches itself to Laurel & Hardy, and when they hear later that it has been stolen, or so the owner believes, and that he is promising dire consequences to the thieves, they are afraid to return it. Accordingly they take it to their little furnished room, despite a strict "no pets" ruling, and do their unsuccessful best to hide it from the landlord.

Laurel & Hardy's last complete silent film, *Angora Love* is fast-paced and full of good individual gags. One of the funniest occurs as Hardy is giving the goat a much-needed bath (in a tub in the middle of the floor) when there is a knock at the door from the suspicious landlord. Instantly, Hardy removes and hides the goat, and to justify the presence of the tub of soapy water, promptly thrusts Laurel's head into it. The gag is repeated later when the bathing attempt is being made a second time, and once more the suspicious landlord knocks on the door. This time

Laurel takes the initiative, even though it is too late, for the landlord has already entered and seen all. But Stan's mind, unable to comprehend all of this, merely reacts instinctively: he removes the goat from the suds, places it on the floor, and energetically shoves Hardy's head beneath the now much dirtier water to give *it* a scrubbing.

The comedians used the basic idea again in their later three-reeler, *The Chimp*—although the individual gags were different—and remade it in toto, with exactly duplicated gags, in *Laughing Gravy,* in which a rather endearing little puppy replaced the goat. Incidentally, stills exist of *Angora Love* showing Laurel and Hardy in an apparent comedy sequence with cameraman George Stevens, but since no such sequence appears in the film it is a matter for conjecture as to whether it was ever shot or was just posed for publicity stills.

Unaccustomed as We Are

HAL ROACH—M-G-M, 1929. *Two reels. Directed by Lewis Foster. Story by Leo McCarey.*
With Laurel & Hardy, Mae Busch, Thelma Todd, Edgar Kennedy.

When Ollie brings Stan home for a meal he has assured him his wife will be delighted to cook, Mrs. Hardy leaves in a huff. The friendly blonde next door, wife of a jealous policeman (Edgar Kennedy) takes pity and cooks dinner for them. In the process she burns her dress, which of course she has to remove just as her husband and Mrs. Hardy return together. She hides in a trunk, and Kennedy, sensing the boys' predicament, and not above a little playing around himself, has the boys bring the trunk over to

his apartment. When the trunk is opened, *both* husbands get it in the neck amid a shower of pots, pans and household furnishings.

Unaccustomed As We Are was Laurel & Hardy's first full talkie, with no silent version issued. Hence its title, even though they certainly had spoken on the screen before. Its plot was transferred intact to provide the last quarter of their much later feature, *Blockheads,* where it was frankly much funnier. Aside from the joys always inherent in Hardy's never-ending battle with his wives, it was fairly dull stuff, though in its use of sound it made further advances over *A Perfect Day* in that it used exaggerated sound effects to suggest off-screen action, a device that they were to use more and more in their upcoming films.

Hollywood Review of 1929

M-G-M, 1929. *Thirteen reels. No individual director credit.*

With an all-star cast, including Buster Keaton, Charles King, Marie Dressler, John Gilbert, Norma Shearer, Lionel Barrymore, Laurel & Hardy.

Musical revue without a plot.

In 1929, all of the major companies jumped on the joint band-wagons of sound and Technicolor to offer revue films featuring all of their contract players. (During the years of World War II, the formula was repeated in films like *Thank Your Lucky Stars, Star Spangled Rhythm* and many others—no more successfully). One would have expected M-G-M, the biggest studio and the one with the biggest stars, to have turned out the best revue film of all, but surprisingly it was but little better than Warner Brothers' very disappointing *The Show of Shows,* and not to be compared with the one that was easily the best and slickest of them all, *Paramount on Parade.* Curiously, the M-G-M revue seemed to assign most of its stars to do the things that they *didn't* do best, and only singer Charles King and comics Laurel & Hardy were really seen to advantage. The comedians' material was not exactly inspired, but it was one of the highlights of a generally disappointing show. Hardy was a magician, Laurel his assistant—inevitably ruining the tricks, or giving away the secret behind them. Jack Benny, as master of ceremonies, was marginally involved in their sequence. Technicolor was reserved for highlights and musical numbers, and much of this color footage has now "hypoed" out of existence in the original negative; fortunately the Laurel & Hardy material was in black and white and has been safely preserved.

With Leo Willis (left foreground) and other toughs en route to jail.

Hoosegow

HAL ROACH—M-G-M, 1929. *Two reels. Directed by James Parrott. Story by Leo McCarey.*
With Laurel & Hardy, James Finlayson, Tiny Sanford, Leo Willis, Dick Sutherland.

Laurel & Hardy are newly arrived convicts, terrified both of their tough cohorts and the prospect of years behind the bars. An attempted escape fails, and they are put to work with a road gang. Told to chop wood for a fire, Laurel hacks down a tree—which happens to have a lookout post built in its uppermost branches, and soon tree, lookout post and guard come crashing down right on the camp's cook-tent.

Society matrons, anxious to see some good in *all* convicts, are unimpressed by Laurel & Hardy's roadgang manner.

An attempted escape in the car of James Finlayson and Tiny Sanford is foiled by a barrel of whitewash.

Put to work digging ditches where they can do no more damage, they accidentally rip a jagged hole in the radiator of prison-inspector James Finlayson's car. To cover up the damage, they stuff rice into the radiator. But as soon as the water in the radiator begins to boil, a veritable volcanic eruption of soggy rice explodes from the car, and soon Finlayson, convicts, guards, and the two dignified matrons who have come along to inspect prison conditions, are engaged in an all-out rice-throwing battle.

Hoosegow is rather too much the formula as before and decidedly unoriginal. The best gags had been used to better effect earlier (the final battle is a re-working of the pie fight, and a sequence with soup originated in *You're Darn Tootin'),* the editing is clumsy, and the use of sound uninspired. It has a great deal of energy, and except for some brief Black Maria scenes takes place entirely out of doors, which gives the various gags more variety of background. A funny, but decidedly below-average short.

Night Owls

HAL ROACH—M-G-M, 1930. *Two reels. Directed by James Parrott. Story by Leo McCarey.*
With Laurel & Hardy, Edgar Kennedy, Anders Randolph.

Hoboes Laurel & Hardy run afoul of cop Edgar Kennedy, who refuses to let them sleep peacefully on a park bench. However, he is in trouble too, and offers to help them if they'll help him. He has been unable to put a stop to a series of robberies on his beat, and

he's in the doghouse with his chief—who, incidentally, lives in a house within the area under Kennedy's "protection." If Laurel & Hardy will attempt to break into and rob the chief's house, he, Kennedy, will rout them. They'll get away scot-free, with a little something for their trouble, and he'll be in solid with the chief again. Not unexpectedly, everything goes wrong, and all three of them wind up under arrest.

Another minor comedy with too many protracted gags—Laurel & Hardy trying to break into the house,

"Just do like I say and it can't miss!"

climbing through windows and already opened doors, locking themselves out after gaining entry, and other time-consuming routines. Even with a paucity of material Laurel & Hardy could be and were funny, but their first talkies had been too slow, even allowing for their deliberate methods, and they seemed to be having a hard time hitting their stride again.

The trash can and the empty tins are a sure tip-off that Oliver's "Shhh!" is in vain.

Police chief Anders Randolf (in pajamas) is unconvinced by Edgar Kennedy's explanation."

Blotto

HAL ROACH–M-G-M, 1930. *Two reels. Directed by James Parrott. Story by Leo McCarey. With Laurel & Hardy, Dorothy Christie.*

Laurel & Hardy decide to play truant from their wives, taking with them a bottle of "the real stuff" to put the finishing touch on their night-club outing—it was Prohibition of course, and genuine liquor was unavailable at a night club. Mrs. Hardy overhears, empties the liquor down the drain, and replaces it with a foul but decidedly non-alcoholic concoction of her own. Delighting in their triumph, the boys get riotously "drunk" at the night club. Their festivities are capped by the ultimate arrival of Mrs. Hardy with the inevitable shot-gun, one blast from which totally demolishes the auto in which they are trying to make their escape.

Still slow, but a decided improvement on its predecessors, *Blotto* is a generally quite satisfactory exploitation of a single situation that the comedians were very fond of re-using and embellishing (*Their Purple Moment, Sons of the Desert, We Faw Down*). It's really little more than a two-man show for most of the proceedings, as they proceed to get howling drunk on their liquor and engage in horse-play with waiters, night club customers and entertainers. Here they also use for the first time in sound their "laughing" routine, in which self-satisfied chuckles at their own cleverness build into an uncontrollable paroxysm of hysterical laughter. There's a priceless moment when they are confronted by Mrs. Hardy, and between gasps and peals of laughter, Hardy explains how they have outwitted her. Whereupon Mrs. Hardy tells how *she* poured the real liquor away. There's a curiously pathetic moment in which Hardy's face registers both doubt and disgust, *and* the realization that his entire evening of drunken behavior was the result of a kind of wishful thinking coupled with self-hypnosis. It's a beautifully subtle as well as funny moment, a worthy climax to a generally underplayed comedy in which the only traditional slapstick sight gag is the fadeout wrap-up of the collapsing automobile.

Rogue Song

M-G-M, 1930. *Eleven reels, in Technicolor. Directed by Lionel Barrymore. Based on Franz Lehar's operetta "Gypsy Love." Scenario by Frances Marion and John Colton. Camera: Percy Hilburn.*

Starring Lawrence Tibbett and Catherine Dale Owen, with Laurel & Hardy.

Tibbett is a Russian bandit king who falls in love with a princess. Her brother has betrayed Tibbett's sister. In revenge, he kills him, at the same time abducting the princess. She escapes, has him arrested and flogged, but then realizes that she loves him after all.

Purely a vehicle for Metropolitan Opera star Lawrence Tibbett, who was never to become a very satisfying screen personality, *Rogue Song* was finished and ready for release when Laurel & Hardy were added as an afterthought to give the film both comedy relief and a measure of box-office insurance. They were billed last in the cast without any kind of "guest star" status, and their material, constructed neither by them nor by their standard Hal Roach writers, was lame, obvious stuff. Lionel Barrymore, a good but stolid director of straight dramatic fare, had neither the flair for *Rogue Song* frou-frou nor for sight comedy, and undoubtedly could do nothing to help them overcome the mediocrity of their material. Their footage was spotted throughout the film, which received only moderate reviews for its values as an operetta and no acclaim at all for its comedy. At best the Laurel & Hardy presence was noted and their comedy relief in a rather turgid film appreciated. However, critical appreciation of Laurel & Hardy was late in arriving, and their mere presence in an allegedly highbrow film of this nature may have been resented by many of the critics, so quite possibly their sequences may have been a good deal better than either memory or contemporary reviews indicate. This is only conjecture, however, since no prints of the film are known to have survived. M-G-M, the producing company, no longer has either a print or a negative of the subject, decomposition having been hastened by the unstable nature of the early Technicolor nitrate celluloid. If a print should suddenly appear, it will be from an unlikely and unpredictable source, probably European. In the meantime, *Rogue Song* holds the dubious distinction of being the only Laurel & Hardy *feature* believed to be no longer in existence, and while it is undoubtedly unrepresentative of their work, one would still give much to see it again, since in it, presumably, one can trace the roots of their own later burlesque operettas *(Fra Diavolo, The Bohemian Girl, Babes in Toyland)* done very much under their own, and Hal Roach's control.

Stan and Oliver steal a scene from Lawrence Tibbett.

The wives are unconvinced by Hardy's sudden headache.

Be Big

HAL ROACH—M-G-M, 1930. *Three reels. Directed by James Parrott.*
   With Laurel & Hardy, Anita Garvin.

During their wives' absence, Laurel & Hardy look forward to taking part in a convention at Atlantic City. They never make it as far as the front door of their home.

Despite the apparent over-simplification of the "story," the above is really all the plot that *Be Big* can boast. Similar in structure to their *A Perfect Day,* it has far less incident and variety, and indeed rapidly becomes rather tiresome. One rather charming joke at the beginning has Laurel, child-like, packing his toy boat to take along to the sea. Thereafter, however, they introduce the one basic joke and play it for far more than it is worth, especially since this is a three-reeler. The required garb for their convention is riding habit. Not only have they not worn

it since the previous convention, but they also contrive to get their outfits mixed up. The bulk of the footage is devoted to Hardy painfully getting into Laurel's too-small pants and boots, and then as laboriously trying to extricate himself from them. One of their weakest films.

The troublesome boots that consume most of the film's running time.

Brats

HAL ROACH—M-G-M, 1930. *Two reels. Directed by James Parrott. Story by Leo McCarey. With Laurel & Hardy.*

With the wives away for the evening, Laurel & Hardy (seemingly living in the same house, in a *ménage á quatre!*) act as baby sitters for their own sons—also played by themselves.

A tremendous improvement on their sound comedies to date, *Brats* marks a turning point in their career. From now on, despite the occasional disap-

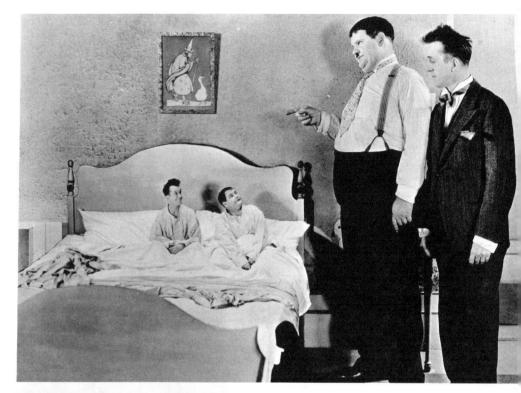

pointments, they can certainly be said to have hit their stride again. *Brats* has absolutely no plot, but is a beautifully conceived vehicle which allows them to display petulantly childish traits as the adults, and shrewdly observed genuinely childish traits as their own offspring. While the adults try vainly to play pool downstairs, the children indulge in horseplay upstairs. Hardy Jr., true to his heritage, "informs" on his pal and tries to pass on the blame for his own misdeeds. Hardy Sr. takes the inevitable fall on a loose roller skate to dive headlong down the stairs to an offscreen collision heralded by reverberating sound effects. The trick photography is unusually carefully done (especially for a Laurel & Hardy film, where the post-George Stevens films were often rather carelessly shot, even to leaving photographic equipment standing or lying within range of the cameras!) and the building of over-scale sets to emphasize the diminutive size of the brats, quite on a par with that in M-G-M's later fantasy film *The Devil Doll*. The best gags are reserved for the end when, with increasing vehemence, Hardy lullabies the youngsters to sleep with "Go to sleep, my babies," only to have them awaken with a start when Laurel steps on a horn, or when Hardy Jr. decides he wants a drink of water. Laurel Sr. goes to the bathroom to oblige, but Hardy Sr. stops him with an imperious gesture. *"You* might spill it!" he chides, opening the bathroom door to be met with a veritable Niagara, which floods the entire apartment. (During their pre-bedtime games, the brats had left the bathroom tap running!)

Note the portrait of Jean Harlow next to the clock.

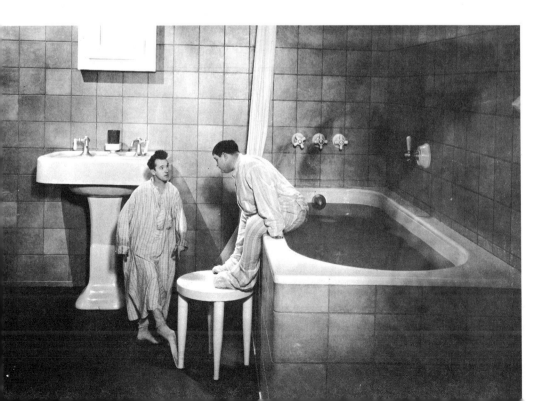

Below Zero

HAL ROACH—M-G-M, 1930. *Two reels. Directed by James Parrott. Story by Leo McCarey. Camera: George Stevens.*
  With Laurel & Hardy, Charles Hall.

Laurel & Hardy are street musicians, whose rendering of "In The Good Old Summertime" on accordion and bassoon during a snowstorm wins them neither friends nor monetary reward. Frustration follows frustration, until finally their instruments are kicked into the street and, on cue, demolished by a passing truck. Cold and hungry, they have the good fortune to find a wallet in the street, and rush into a nearby eatery. Ordering a sumptuous meal, and anxious to share their good fortune, they invite the local policeman to join them as their guest. Graciously he acquiesces—but when the bill is presented, it develops

that the wallet they have found is *his*. Attempting to escape his wrath, Hardy hides in a trash can, and is collected by the garbage truck; Laurel hides in a rain-barrel, from which he emerges, grotesquely bloated, having drunk all the water.

A curious, bizarre, almost surrealist comedy, *Below Zero* is methodically paced (without being slow) and almost without dialogue until the closing sequence in the restaurant, where Hardy orders the most succulent of dishes and engages in bantering small talk with the cop. The early exchanges with non-music-lovers in the street (one of them is an elderly lady who smashes a milk bottle on Hardy's head, and destroys his accordion) are likewise largely silent. Yet it is a situational rather than a sight-gag comedy, one of their oddest, and if not one of their funniest, then certainly one of their cleverest.

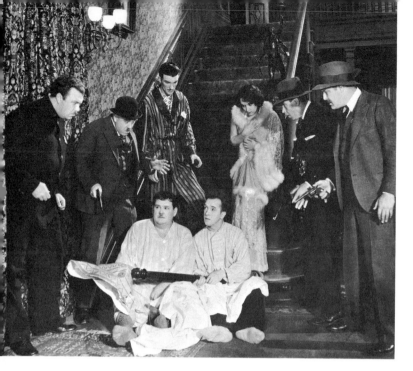

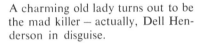
A charming old lady turns out to be the mad killer — actually, Dell Henderson in disguise.

The Laurel & Hardy Murder Case

HAL ROACH—M-G-M, 1930. *Three reels. Directed by James Parrott.*

    With Laurel & Hardy, Fred Kelsey, Stanley Blystone, Dell Henderson, Tiny Sanford.

Hardy learns that Laurel has inherited a fortune, and a little reluctantly taking Mr. Laurel with him, goes to claim it. The old house in which he finds himself is frightening indeed, but conditions of the will demand that they stay there overnight. The house appears to be full of killers and ghosts, and just as Hardy is about to meet his end, he wakes up. It has all been a dream.

Although most of the straight old-house horror chillers of the late 20's and early 30's—and especially *The Cat and the Canary, The Bat Whispers* and *The Old Dark House*—stand up very well today, with their evocative mood photography and stylish sets, the comedy thrillers in the same genre (*The Gorilla*) tend to date rather badly. This Laurel & Hardy film, not only a comedy but also a deliberate spoof of a then-popular genre, tends to date even more. The slow pace, minus the style of a director like Leni or Whale, produces lethargy rather than tension; and all the time-honored clutching-hand and disappearing-body routines have since become such clichés that burlesques of them date even more than the real thing. For a comedy, too, *The Laurel & Hardy Murder Case* is often surprisingly grim, the mortality rate, the screams, the grotesque faces, often seem so close to the authentic article that, despite being deliberately overdone, they are just not funny. Many of the gags—a bat that gets caught in a pillow case and flies, a white phantom, through the house—have too mechanical a quality, and the dream ending is decidedly unsatisfactory since it comes at a time when no other solution would be possible (unlike, for example, the dream endings of *The Chase* and *The Woman in the Window,* which resolve their problems *before* the trick revelation). The funniest moments occur at the beginning of the film when Hardy, who has just finished putting Laurel in his place once more, suddenly discovers the Laurel inheritance and hastily tries to re-ingratiate himself with his friend to ensure a share in the fortune.

102

Hog Wild

HAL ROACH—M-G-M, 1930. *Two reels. Directed by James Parrott. Story by Leo McCarey. With Laurel & Hardy, Fay Holderness.*

First at the prodding of his wife, and then to assert his authority when she demands that he stop, Hardy —with the help of Mr. Laurel—tries to erect a radio aerial on the roof of his home.

One of their finest examples of sustained slapstick, *Hog Wild* gives Laurel & Hardy something of an affinity with Buster Keaton as they struggle manfully but unsuccessfully with an inanimate and basically simple mechanical prop—a radio aerial. Laurel's proffered help is accepted somewhat dubiously. "Well, all right, if you'll really *help* me!" agrees Hardy, his expression showing all too clearly that he realizes what a mistake his decision is. Following orders, Laurel brings his car around to the side of the house, honking his horn to signal his arrival, the noise so unnerving Mr. Hardy (by now halfway up a ladder) that he, his apparatus, and the ladder come thundering to the ground instantly! No problem in constructing an aerial (so that Mrs. Hardy can get China) is overlooked. Hammerings on the roof result in large pieces of plaster falling unerringly from the ceiling below onto Mrs. Hardy's head; invariably the wrong extension is plugged into the wrong electrical socket, resulting in sparks, explosions and howls of pain, and on one occasion Mr. Hardy is jerked down the chimney to arrive in the hearth at Mrs. Hardy's feet in a shower of soot and bricks.

Sitting there patiently, like an out-of-season Santa Claus, waiting for the final brick which must fall on his already battered head in a few moments, Hardy invokes not sympathy from his wife but short-tempered impatience. More in concern for her house than his health, she tells him to forget it, that she'll get a qualified man for the job. "Not on your *life*," retorts the now-determined Hardy, who goes aloft once more to prove that he can do anything he sets his mind to. Nestled on the front lawn, close to the house, is a rustic little fish pond, neatly fringed with ferns and lilies. It sits there almost malignantly, a destiny that Hardy has no hope of avoiding. Sure

One of the many falls into the pond: In the film itself, the camera concentrates on the boys, and this wider angle shot reveals an extra standing in for Fay Holderness, who played the wife. British documentary-maker Basil Wright, much impressed with the variations of this running gag, waxed enthusiastic about the Eisenstein-like use of a flight of birds for the final plunge. Alas, Mr. Wright was suffering from a rose-colored memory or wishful thinking, since there is no such scene in the film.

enough, up on the roof Laurel pulls too soon on some wiring, and Hardy trips, rolls down the slanted roof, and disappears over the side to an off-screen splash and those inevitable hurled buckets of water. Down below in the pond, Hardy sits dejectedly, yet patiently. He squeezes the last drop of water from one gloved finger, then another, flicks a drop from his sodden overalls, and wades ashore to start all over again.

The fall into the water soon becomes the running gag of the middle portion of the film—the end result always the same, the manner and the means always different. Mrs. Hardy, watching from behind a curtain, is allowed a rare moment of humanity—she almost, but not quite, stifles a smile which indicates a kind of warm affection for her husband's bumbling stupidity. It is about the closest that a Hardy wife ever came to showing understanding and even loving tolerance for her mate. The moment is over and is never repeated, but it is a touch of subtlety perfectly placed in a story-line where Hardy is suffering as never before merely for the comfort and convenience of his wife. The work, however, never *is* quite finished; Hardy is half-way up a ladder which, for added height, has been propped on the back seat of Laurel's car. Inadvertently Laurel releases the brake, and the car goes careening off into the busy streets of Culver City with Hardy still perched precariously on top. It's an expert piece of fast-action slapstick, the kind of stunt comedy more normally associated with Sennett than Roach. The hairbreadth escapes from collisions, the juggling of the ladder to bend it forward as they go under a low bridge, the weaving in and out of traffic, all of these familiar but always reliable gags are done with verve and finesse, and yet it is still the pantomimic reactions from Hardy that produce the funniest scenes. As Laurel's car passes a parked open-topped bus, the ladder, now at a 45-degree angle, scrapes along the top of the bus. But Hardy's reaction is one of embarrassment rather than self-preservation. His automatic response is to raise his bowler hat to the startled passengers in the bus, and to stammer a few words of apology for the astonishing spectacle he presents. By the time thoughts of scram-

bling to safety reach him, it is too late—the ladder has been dragged to the front of the bus, and no longer supported by it, nosedives spectacularly to the ground. Even here, spreadeagled and battered on the ground, Hardy gets no sympathy from a hostile world. Seconds after the fall, the bus driver is impatient to be on his way; he gives his horn a warning toot and starts up. Barely managing to roll out of the way, Hardy is greeted by another honking horn and is almost run over by a truck. Safely back on the sidewalk, shivering with terror, he is met by his wife who is crying and badly upset. "I'm all right, honey," he soothes her, all of his suffering worthwhile if it has kindled a spark of concern in his wife. But he is denied even this balm: contemptuously she tells him that she isn't crying over *him*, but because the man from the finance company came to take the radio away. Defeated, he, his wife and Stan prepare to drive home. But now it's the auto's turn to have the last word. It refuses to budge, although as Stan pulls lever after lever, and presses button after button, it offers a series of shattering explosions which reduce Mr. Hardy's nerves to an even more ragged state. From behind, a streetcar comes clanging along at a furious rate, evidently with no intention of stopping. Horrified spectators avert their eyes in terror as we hear a mighty off-screen collision. Then—back to the ultimate frustration—the car twisted like a pretzel into a semi-circle. It now runs—but only in the same never-ending circle that goes nowhere and gets nowhere.

Now more than thirty-five years old, *Hog Wild* is as fresh and undated as ever. The superbly executed sight gags naturally dominate, yet there is still time to give the characters slightly more dimension than usual. For all her shrewishness, the wife *does* have a sense of humor, and Hardy, undeniably henpecked, still cares for her and seeks to please her. As for Laurel, he's human enough this time to be enticed by the pretty legs of a shapely girl as she crosses a puddle—and almost to wreck his car as a result. Carefully built as always, but jam-packed with incident, *Hog Wild* is easily one of the best Laurel & Hardy subjects.

Another Fine Mess

HAL ROACH—M-G-M, 1930. *Three reels. Directed by James Parrott.*

With Laurel & Hardy, Thelma Todd, James Finlayson.

Wealthy big-game hunter Finlayson takes off on a vacation, leaving to his butler and maid the task of renting his mansion while he's away. Glad to see the back of him, his far from loyal servants leave as soon as his taxi has taken him to the docks. Laurel & Hardy, fleeing from a policeman, find in the deserted mansion an ideal refuge—and since the policeman maintains his vigil outside, they are forced to remain there. A crusty British aristocrat and his sexy American wife come to take up residence in answer to Finlayson's ad, and in order to stay in their safe refuge, Hardy masquerades as the owner of the house, and Laurel as his maid. Despite some bad slip-ups, Hardy's aplomb carries the day—until Finlayson, having forgotten something, returns from the boat, is flabbergasted by the situation confronting him, and summons the police. Laurel & Hardy, dis-guised as one of his trophies—a horned goat—make their escape on a bicycle, the police in hot pursuit.

Although the three-reel length seems hardly justified, some better than average situational humor (slapstick is at a minimum), good dialogue, Hardy's smooth savoir-faire as the bogus huntsman-millionaire, and Laurel's dame masquerade more than carry the day. Hardy's small talk about big game hunting and his inability to find his way about his own house works well with the traditional "silly ass Englishman" opposite number. Laurel, called upon to make so many quick changes from "butler" to "maid" that there are occasional overlappings of costume, has one excellent sequence where he settles down to some "girl talk" with the young bride. The dialogue here, pungent and more than a little risqué, with Laurel covering up one faux-pas by a worse one, is markedly better than usual. Despite the preponderance of plot and dialogue, the film moves well and the climactic gag with the apparent bicycle-riding goat pursued by fearful police is a bizarre episode that might well have been explored even further.

Chickens Come Home

HAL ROACH—M-G-M, 1931. *Three reels. Directed by James Horne.*

   With Laurel & Hardy, Mae Busch, James Finlayson.

Hardy, a newly married and newly successful businessman, is suddenly visited by an old flame from the past, who threatens blackmail. Stan, his friend and business associate, is told to keep the vamp at bay—but she descends on the Hardy home nevertheless, and the complications that ensue defy a logical explanation to the automatically suspicious Mrs. Hardy.

A meticulous re-working of *Love 'Em and Weep,* one of the earlier films in which they appeared together (though not as a team), *Chickens Come Home* is a fine example of Laurel & Hardy's control over their own work, and of the sophistication they could bring to basically knockabout material. Although there are one or two fine sight-gags, the comedy is again largely situational. One of the well-developed gags common to both versions is of the wife's arrival in her husband's office while the vamp is hiding in the bathroom. The silent version handled it all as a good, if unsubtle, visual gag; the sound equivalent tones down the rather outlandish elements of the vamp hiding, and concentrates more on the husband's efforts to keep his wife *out* of the bathroom. When he finally succeeds, and Mrs. Hardy is about to be eased out of the office, Laurel breaks in with "Wouldn't you like to wash your hands before you go?" Hardy essays what was originally the James Finlayson role; Laurel repeats as the friend; and Finlayson here is cast as Hardy's butler, a nebulous role for Charlie Hall in the original. The expanded part in this new version gives Finlayson some fine opportunities to vary his traditional relationship with Hardy. Always his enemy, he was also usually his social or official superior—an Army officer, a wealthy employer, a man of property. As the butler, he still manages to be Hardy's superior, for in overhearing Hardy's compromising phone calls, he is put into a unique position for blackmailing. With a knowing wink at the audience and a scowl of disapproval for his employer, he manages to be on hand whenever the phone rings, hand outstretched for the bribe which *may* ensure his silence. One of the better Laurel & Hardy films of its period, its only real flaw is its padded length; indeed, of all their three-reelers, only *The Music Box* really justifies the extra reel.

Opportunistic Finlayson sees blackmail possibilities in Hardy's mysterious feminine caller.

Mae Busch and "another fine mess" in the making.

Laughing Gravy

HAL ROACH—M-G-M, 1931. *Two reels. Directed by James Horne.*
   With Laurel & Hardy, Charles Hall.

Concealing a dog in their apartment against the landlord's orders, Laurel and Hardy are forced to eject him into the snow when he is discovered—and spend most of the night trying to bring him in again. Their efforts make a shambles of their apartment and they *and* the dog are about to be ejected—permanently—when their apartment building is quarantined for smallpox. The landlord commits suicide, and the boys remove their hats respectfully, but not with too much indication of genuine remorse.

An exact re-working of *Angora Love, Laughing Gravy* repeats all of its best gags and extends its violence. Placing it all in a wintry setting, with much of the action taking place on the snow-covered roof in a howling storm, gives it a little more point and substance than the original, too. Everyone suffers spectacularly with the exception of the dog, Laughing Gravy, the cause of it all. Despite his small size and helpless appearance, he seems quite happy when thrust out into the cold, and wags his tail briskly at each and every misfortune that befalls his would-be rescuers. If some of the nocturnal prowlings are a bit too protracted, there is still a remarkable variety of violent action: Hardy sliding off the slippery roof and into a freezing rain-barrel; he and Mr. Laurel settling down to a peaceful sleep in a bed which promptly collapses under them (a periodic gag of theirs) in the process also sending large chunks of plaster down on the sleeping landlord on the floor below; and a long sequence in which the boys, given an hour to pack up and get out of their apartment, try to clean up and somehow manage only to bring down disaster on disaster upon their heads. Hardy nose-dives from a cake of soap; both are covered with soot, and in trying to wash up, merely add to the mess. The landlord too—Charlie Hall at his best, here sporting an obnoxious little moustache, and a huge bump on his head from a Laurel & Hardy-provoked accident—winds up soaked, battered, dirtied, and finally dead by his own hand! Ranging from the gentle humors of Laurel's hiccups (which start the dog barking, thus setting off the series of chain reactions) to the spectacular and almost choreographed gags with the washtub (described in some detail in the notes on *Angora Love*), *Laughing Gravy* offers a fine array of both typical and well-executed Laurel & Hardy material. There's little in it that they didn't do better somewhere else, but the sheer virtuosity of it all and the undistilled concentration on Laurel & Hardy (apart from Hall and a brief appearance by a drunk, there are no other characters in the film) make it one of the most enjoyable, if not one of the most notable, of all their shorts.

Our Wife

HAL ROACH—M-G-M, 1931. *Two reels. Directed by James Horne.*

With Laurel & Hardy, James Finlayson, Ben Turpin.

Millionaire James Finlayson is more than eager to get his rotund and rather silly daughter married and off his hands—but he does draw the line at Oliver Hardy as a son-in-law. The marriage forbidden, Hardy takes matters into his own hands and stages an elopement. Despite the assistance of Laurel, who would ring the doorbell to inform the prospective bride that all is in readiness for the secret getaway, the escape and the marriage finally come off—except that the minister is cross-eyed Ben Turpin, and it is Laurel who emerges as the bridegroom.

A rather intriguing comedy this, for it mixes traditional Laurel & Hardy material with some (for them) decidedly off-beat gags. The opening sequences are delightful, inter-cutting between the happy sighs of the intended mates, and showing the crosses that each of them has to bear. Finlayson, the bride's father, takes one look at a photo of Ollie, and locks his daughter into her room, prior to tripping on a carpet sweeper and making a spectacular headlong flight down the stairs. Hardy, likewise a picture of joy, has to put up not only with Stan's usual ineptitudes (off to a good start by inadvertently ripping

Hardy's pants) but with his interested eavesdropping on the pre-wedding billing and cooing over the telephone. After much blowing of kisses and exchanges of endearments, Hardy and his girl friend finally make their goodbyes, and Laurel adds his own cheery "goodbye" as they hang up. Particularly amusing, if a trifle distasteful, is Laurel's handling of the wedding cake. A swarm of flies, attracted by the icing, alight on the cake and begin the feasting early. The sound track gives each fly a nauseously exaggerated voice, something of a cross between a buzz-saw and a dive bomber. Helpful Laurel promptly attacks the invaders with his insect-killing Flit spray, each execution being duly recorded by an equally exaggerated pop, until the corpses of the flies make the wedding repast most unappetizing indeed. The elopement sequence is a typical episode of frustrations and simplicities made difficult: a ringing doorbell and the noisy dropping of the escape ladder instantly waking the household; Hardy collapsing under the weight of his bride-to-be and the luggage she heaves out of her window; and Laurel thoughtfully and noisily pelting the loving couple with rice. Thereafter it goes into a long but generally effective Marx Brothers-like sequence, although in fairness it must be pointed out that it pre-dates by several years the sequences in *A Night at the Opera* and *At the Circus* that it most resembles. Laurel, having been entrusted with the task of providing the getaway transportation, has produced the tiniest of midget cars into which Laurel, Hardy, the bride and several pieces of bulky luggage must be squeezed. So impossible does such a maneuver look that one suspects that perspectives must have been changed throughout the routine, with gradually larger prop cars being introduced as more and more flesh is forced into such a confined space. The routine works well, but it is a gag of frustration and growing exasperation, almost too convincing and too near possibility to be as funny as it should be. The Marx Brothers, in handling the same situation, added speed, insanity, a variety of gags, and a steady progression of large and absurdly unnecessary characters inching their way into the same tiny space. The basic joke in *Our Wife* is established instantly, and thereafter is stretched rather than developed. However, it is far funnier and better executed than the similar upper-berth gag that they used on occasion, and while it is the longest single gag in the film, it is still not dragged out beyond its comedy value.

Come Clean

HAL ROACH—M-G-M, 1931. *Two reels. Directed by James Horne.*
   With Laurel & Hardy, Mae Busch, Gertrude Astor, Charlie Hall.

The Hardys, enjoying a quiet day at home, have their rare moment of bliss shattered by a social call from the Laurels. Stanley wants some ice cream, and while he and Ollie are out to buy it, they rescue a suicide (Mae Busch) from the river. Far from grateful, and clearly a lady of questionable morals, she tells them, "Now you've saved me, you have to take care of me!" Against their better judgment, the boys conceal her in their bathroom at home, but the wives gradually become suspicious of the presence of another woman. Just as all seems lost, the police come to arrest her, for she is an escaped lunatic. Since Hardy has carefully placed all the blame for her presence on Laurel, it is Laurel who gets the reward for her capture.

A curious mixture of some of the best and some of the lesser Laurel & Hardy, *Come Clean* is an uneven film with a good deal of borrowing from earlier ones. The whole opening sequence is a repetition, and an improvement on, the opening of *Should Married Men Go Home?* The bantering sweet nothings exchanged between Mr. and Mrs. Hardy are a sheer delight. Hardy, in one of his tragically rare moments of marital bliss, being at complete peace with the world as he smiles coyly at his wife, traces delicate little designs on the tablecloth with his forefinger, exchanges coquettish flattery, and happily tells Mrs. Hardy that they can be alone all day, "with nothing to mar our joy." Whereupon the door bell rings, and hastily reverting to type, Mrs. Hardy (Gertrude

"We'll pretend we're not in," says Ollie to wife Gertrude Astor.

Astor) stalks away in disgust with a snarled remark about "those Laurels."

Hardy is reluctant to give up his day of connubial bliss so easily. "We'll pretend we're not in." Laurel is persistent, and continues to ring the doorbell until his impatient wife yanks him away. But first he writes a note and places it under the door. Hardy, standing guard on the other side, sees it and promptly picks it up. Deducing that someone must be home after all, Laurel renews his assault on the doorbell, and Hardy, realizing his error, hastily shoves the note *back* under the door to Laurel, who is bemused rather than in-

sulted by the whole affair. Inside, the Hardys stand quarrelling in whispers while the indiscreet door slowly opens of its own accord. Delighted that his friend is in after all, and still not grasping the situation, Laurel grins in pleasure. Their backs to the door, the Hardys turn around and make the best of a horrible situation. "Well, well, well, well, well!" beams Hardy in mock surprise, twiddling his tie to cover his embarrassment, while Mrs. Hardy grits her teeth and forces an effusively friendly welcome to Mrs. Laurel.

After such a promising start, beautifully timed and played, and agonizingly close to reality, the film tends to move in jerks. Laurel goes out for ice cream, can't get what he wants, and has to call back for instructions until his last nickel has gone, whereupon Hardy has to rush out to his rescue. Asking for a list of what the ice cream sales clerk (Charlie Hall) *hasn't* got, trying to salvage some flavors that appeal to him from the ice cream that *is* available, unconsciously playing with a container of straws and dropping them all over the floor, Laurel is again the infant nuisance; Hardy the protecting father-figure who, all humility and apologies, calms the ruffled feathers and shattered nerves of the ice cream man. It's a fine comedy sequence, but the change from two husbands and buddies to an adult-child relationship is too sudden, and there is a further change when the Mae Busch episode (deriving from the basic plot-line of *Love 'Em and Weep*) gets under way. The by-play of the rescue is amusing, Hardy's eloquent *preparations* for a dive to the rescue being climaxed by his horrified reaction when he is accidentally pushed into the river by Laurel. Now the comedians change again, and are once more allied shoulder to shoulder

An attempt, doomed to failure, to buy ice cream from Charlie Hall.

111

An unappreciative Mae Busch tells them: "You saved my life – now look after me!"

A desperate attempt to spirit Mae away before the wives see her.

in the eternal battle against the women. The rescued Mae is vicious, unreasonable, sadistically enjoying the obvious discomfort she is causing them. At first Hardy refuses to be browbeaten; he'll bluff it out, and tell the wives everything. But Mae's mocking laugh only confirms what he already knows—the wives, being women too, are automatically just as unreasonable and will never believe their perfectly honest story. So the impatient Mae, demanding dry clothes and a payoff, is ensconced in their apartment. The attempt to prevent wives and Mae from meeting does produce some genuinely amusing moments: Hardy playing for time by telling risqué jokes and deliberately withholding the punch-lines, and, when Mae begins to scream, Laurel & Hardy's sudden jumping up to stage a mock parade and bang imitation drums to deaden her noise. The climax has its own peculiar charm too. Laurel, sitting fully clothed in a bathtub, is asked how he is going to spend all the money that will come to him as a reward for Mae's capture. "I'm going to buy a thousand dollars' worth of chocolate ice cream," he replies, at which Hardy reaches into the bathtub, pulls out the plug, and with a frightened yelp, accompanied by the gurgling of water, Laurel disappears down the drain— an effect not shown of course, but created by the

soundtrack and the satisfied "You had it coming!" look on Hardy's face as he inspects the now empty tub.

Come Clean starts off with such assurance, and contains such good individual sequences, that it is unfortunate that it is so untidy and disjointed in its construction.

Hardy glances at the audience for its acquiescence, yanks the plug, and Laurel disappears.

Pardon Us

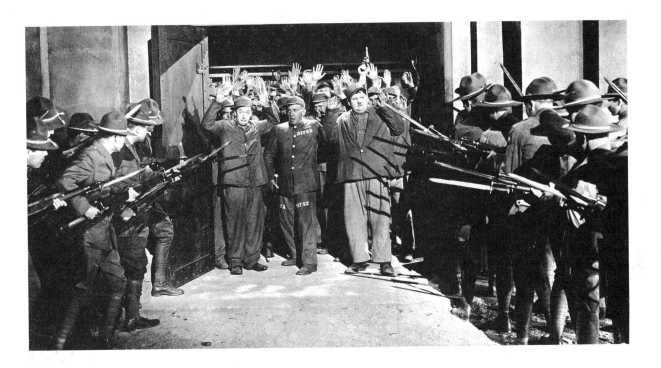

HAL ROACH—M-G-M, 1931. *Six reels. Released in Europe as* GAOL BIRDS. *Directed by James Parrott. Scenario by H. M. Walker. Camera: Jack Stevens.*

With Laurel & Hardy, Wilfred Lucas, June Marlow, James Finlayson, Walter Long, Robert Kortman, Leo Willis.

Imprisoned for illegal beer brewing during the prohibition era, Laurel & Hardy form a strong friendship with the toughest inmate, Walter Long, who mistakes the "razzberry" noise made by Laurel's loose tooth as a sign of courage. Nobody hitherto has ever stood up to him! Inadvertently, however, the boys ruin Long's massive prison-break scheme, though they themselves escape. In black face, they take refuge in a Negro community, and are caught only when Laurel's loose tooth identifies them to the prison warden, whose car has accidentally stalled near the cotton fields where they are working. Back in prison again, they get involved with yet another of Long's mutinies—and this time, though by accident, Laurel's "heroism" is responsible for the quelling of the riot, and the boys are pardoned. As the warden

bids them farewell and hopes that they'll return to the jobs they held before their incarceration, Laurel sees a chance for an immediate turnover and tries to get an advance order from the warden for a keg of beer!

Pardon Us was Laurel & Hardy's first feature-length starring vehicle, and the critical reaction was typical of that to be made of almost all their features from then on: the critics were amused and entertained, but felt that there was too much padding, and that the comedians were much better suited to shorts. It is a curious criticism to have been made, for almost all of their features remained commendably short, usually around the 65-minute mark, even when their full-length features had been established as good box-office, and carried the top half of the bill. Features of six reels gave them time for a semblance of plot line, but also allowed for undistilled Laurel and Hardy material; indeed, their weaker features (*Swiss Miss, Bonnie Scotland*) were those in which they compromised with critical demand for more substance, and added romantic or musical sub-plots which were both intrusive and extraneous. For their

Wilfrid Lucas: "And still they come."

first feature (excluding *Rogue Song,* which was not a vehicle for them) *Pardon Us,* though technically dated today, is remarkably good. Its pacing and editing are admittedly sluggish, reducing the potential of many sequences, but it contains some extremely funny and often imaginative material. Further, it was made at the same time as M-G-M's *The Big House,* and thus gained in production value from the use of that film's big-scale sets, extras, and even out-takes.

Slapstick, situational humor, and violet sight-gags are neatly meshed. There is a beautiful opening se-

quence in which the new convicts are interviewed by the warden, played by Wilfred Lucas, an old Griffith veteran from the Biograph days, whose parodying of the benevolent movie warden revealed an unsuspected flair for comedy. "And still they come . . ." he intones sadly, before giving Laurel & Hardy the standard "welcoming" speech. A prison is a prison he explains gently, rules are rules, and they have to be obeyed. Laurel & Hardy, impressed by his humanity, nod in mute agreement. They will be model prisoners and pay their debt to society. "Obey the rules,"

Posing as Negro cotton-pickers during an escape attempt.

Charlie Hall's expression rather belies his "You won't feel a thing" assurances.

drones on Lucas, "and you'll get along just fine; break them (and here his voice rises to an unexpectedly savage fury) and you'll find this place HELL ON EARTH!" Laurel's promise of good behavior isn't helped by the loose-toothed razzberry that climaxes his sentence, and the pair start out on a more than dubious footing. The loose-tooth gag is used with variations throughout, and even includes a visit to the dentist (in which the sound effects used for the extractions are mercifully unreal, but quite nerve-shattering just the same) which is a revision of their routine in *Leave 'Em Laughing*. A prison-school sequence with Finlayson as the teacher has a nice old vaudeville ring to it, though some of the verbal gags are tipped off too far in advance, and lose punch through the slowness of the cutting. There's one extraordinary gag, quite unlike anything they have ever done, in which the comedians are incarcerated in adjoining solitary confinement cells. For several minutes, the camera holds in one take on an exterior of the dimly lit cells, while the sound track records an insane and irrelevant conversation between the unseen couple, which begins with Laurel asking what time it is, and drifts into a lengthy discussion of food! Another curious highlight occurs after the escape sequence, when the pair has joined the Negro com-

munity. Coming home to their shanty-camp after a hard day's cotton picking, they relax by going into a soft-shoe dance and singing a sentimental Southern song. Such episodes were to be infrequent but cherished moments in a number of their other features, including *Way Out West* and *The Flying Deuces*. There is no dubbing involved, and Hardy's voice is particularly rich and pleasing. The sequences are relaxed and rather warm, placed there without either reason or build-up, almost as though two clowns want to stop being funny for a moment and relive the traditions of vaudeville and music hall that preceded their film work. Although it's a pity that such casual musical charm wasn't used more often in their films, its spontaneity might well have been minimized had such a routine become a "regular" in their inventory.

Though *Pardon Us* must be regarded as one of their lesser features, it nevertheless has a great deal of merit. Its erratic editing may also be the result of wholesale cutting (possibly as their first starring vehicle it may have been planned as an eight- or nine-reeler) for the stills indicate that many sequences never even suggested in the film (including one where they appear as old men in retirement) were shot but jettisoned.

115

One Good Turn

HAL ROACH—M-G-M, 1931. *Two reels. Directed by James Horne.*

With Laurel & Hardy, Mary Carr, James Finlayson, Billy Gilbert.

Victims of the Depression, Laurel & Hardy are travelling the countryside in their battered auto, living in the open. Their meal and much of their limited laundry is ruined when their campfire gets out of hand, and they decide that they'll finally have to throw themselves on the mercy of those more fortunate than they. In a small town, widow Mary Carr takes pity on them—but after being fed by her, they misunderstand some overheard rehearsals for amateur theatrics, and think she is about to be thrown out of her home by mortgage-owner James Finlayson. They head for town, make an impassioned speech, sell their wreck of a car to a drunk, and return with the mortgage money, only to find that their grand gesture is futile.

More contrived in its plotting than most of their shorts, and one of the few to have a genuinely sympathetic female character, in the person of Mary Carr, perennial mother in such silent tear-jerkers as *Over the Hill, One Good Turn* is better in its individual components than in sum total. Hardy's self-pitying little speech about the degradation of being poor is even quite moving, despite the wholly comic framework in which it is placed. The gallantry of his reluctant appeal for charity is neatly counterbalanced by Laurel's matter-of-fact approach to the business at hand. "We are victims of the depression," explains Hardy, "and we haven't eaten for three days." "Three days?" exclaims the kind old lady in horror, and Laurel helpfully adds, "Yes—yesterday, today and tomorrow!" Undismayed, his hands pantomiming the delicate preparation of the simple repast he is asking

The worm turns, as Mary Carr looks on.

for, Hardy continues: "I wonder if we could trouble you for a slice of buttered toast?", while Laurel chimes in, "And while you're at it, could you slap a piece of ham on it?"

Offering to work for their meal, the boys chop a little wood, which presents some slapstick opportunities for hurtling wood, ashcans, and dusty carpets to direct themselves at Mr. Hardy's person. The meal itself, with Hardy's coffee filled with salt, and the elasticized bacon brought into play as a weapon, is another good sight-gag sequence. The play rehearsal episode gives James Finlayson a chance to lampoon his stock performance, which is *already* a lampoon, and for Mary Carr to spoof her former stock in trade. On her knees, she pleads so eloquently for mercy from the hardhearted villain that his trousers are almost dragged to the floor by her over-energetic hand-claspings. The auto sale in the city—the auto of course collapses into rubble as soon as the sale is made—gives Hardy further opportunities for ultra-elaborate theatrics. The best is reserved for the end, however, when Hardy suspects Laurel of having stolen from their benefactress, and in flowery language brushes aside his protestations of innocence, and continues to upbraid him for the depths of depravity to which he has sunk. When the widow confirms that Laurel's innocence is a fact, Hardy's crestfallen smile of apology, and his coy "I made a slight faux-pas" cannot save him. For once Laurel's worm turns. He pokes Hardy in the eye with his finger, kicks him in the shins, and finally takes after him with an axe, cornering him in the garage. "Come out of there!" orders Laurel, like an axe-murdering child; "I won't; you leave me alone!" cringes back Hardy, the bully-child who has finally been beaten by his own victim.

Like so many Laurel & Hardy films, *One Good Turn* starts out with them possessing nothing but a means of transportation and/or livelihood, and winds up with them having lost even that, yet remaining somehow undefeated. In other ways, though, it is one of their less typical works. While not one of their best, it is one of the slickest and smoothest of their early talkies.

Beau Hunks

A spot of home-wrecking before joining the Legion to forget.

Commandant Charles Middleton is unimpressed by their genial attempts to "give notice" — while the continuity girl seems to have been unimpressed by the cameraman's clapper-board left on the desk!

HAL ROACH—M-G-M, 1931. *Four reels. Released in Europe as* BEAU CHUMPS. *Directed by James Horne.*

With Laurel & Hardy, Charles Middleton, Leo Willis.

Laurel & Hardy joins the Foreign Legion to enable Hardy to forget a tragic love affair. But the girl who jilted him seems to have been the sweetheart of all the other Legionnaires—including the Commandant! Reasoning that she is not worth their sacrifice, they announce their intention of resigning, and earn the enmity of their commanding officer. However, they redeem themselves when Riffs attack the fort, and they save the day by sprinkling tacks in the path of the marauding Arabs.

Four reels was a clumsy length for Laurel & Hardy, and they never repeated it. It was not long enough to allow for a story line or to justify worthwhile production values, and at the same time it was far too long for loosely-connected slapstick. In reissue, it was often cut to three and even two reels without any marked effect on continuity. The plot seems to have been inspired by two contemporary films—Von Sternberg's Dietrich-Cooper vehicle *Morocco*, and the Laurence Olivier-Erich von Stroheim *Friends and Lovers*. However, there is no serious attempt to parody any of the eminently spoofable plot elements in those films, and the film is merely a matter of flat, predictable, and very slow-paced slapstick. The opening sequences, when Hardy receives word of his rejection—and wrecks a piano in the process—are the only ones where their material is in any way up to standard.

119

Helpmates

HAL ROACH—M-G-M, 1931. *Two reels. Directed by James Parrott.*
With Laurel & Hardy.

Notified that his wife is coming home a day earlier than expected from a vacation, Hardy calls in his friend Mr. Laurel to help obliterate the evidence of a wild party. Laurel's assistance ultimately results in the loss of Hardy's clothes, his wife, and finally the house itself, which is reduced to a smoking ruin.

Laurel & Hardy's last 1931 release was one of their best from any period, comparing favorably with their silent classics. It was so much a purely two-man show (as Chaplin's *One A.M.* was a one-man show) that one genuinely regrets the fleeting and quite unnecessary appearances of the wife and a messenger boy.

Although the film abounds in fast and often violent slapstick, it is dominated by the single situation of Hardy's attempts to clean up after a wild (but we are sure blameless) wild party. The prevailing mood of

frustration is aided to by Laurel's occasional obstinacy—every so often he rebels against Hardy exploiting him, and at one point asks belligerently, "Who d'you think I am, Cinderella?" Hardy manages to mollify his friend and get him back to work with an appeasing remark which contains veiled insults that continue to work on Laurel through the film. He *thinks* he has been insulted again and is ready to down tools, but he can't be sure so carries on with his tasks. The dialogue between the two, starting with a long telephone conversation and carrying on through their cleaning-up collaboration, has rather more bite than usual, and some rambling, nonsensical discussions that somehow link up to form a kind of logic, as in the earlier Marx Brothers films. There is also more cohesion to the various sight-gags themselves, for each one leads logically to the next, minor accident leading to major disaster, so that the more they try to organize their work, the more they add to the inevitability of their defeat. Hardy being jabbed in the eye as Laurel tries to unstop the sink with a plunger, Hardy sailing gracefully through mid-air as he treads on a cake of soap, Hardy being covered by

120

an avalanche of pots, pans, soot and flour, are but precursors of more elaborate gags in which chain reactions are methodically set in motion. Water thrown at an open window is hurled back at the thrower when the window suddenly slides shut; Hardy goes outside to pry the window open, only to be soaked when Laurel sees the obstacle overcome, and throws the water out again. In rage, Hardy hurls a rock back at Laurel; it misses, but breaks sundry fittings and starts a lamp swinging so that it breaks loose and hurtles through a window, knocking a gardener head over heels, and leaving his garden hose to spray through an open window, so that when Hardy enters in dry clothes, he is immediately soaked again. Attempts to dry and press Hardy's clothes result in them being spoiled beyond hope of salvage. Mrs. Hardy meanwhile is waiting at the station, furious at the delay. Hardy, his last suit now ruined, is too defeated even to be angry—and his frustration is so real that, as he often did in such scenes, he fluffs a line or two of dialogue. Sorrowfully he tells himself in a resigned voice, "It's enough to make a man bust out crying"—and looks to the audience for that surge of sympathy that is most certainly forthcoming. Then—an inspiration. He disappears, to return moments later wearing an old Admiral's uniform, left over from a masquerade. With cocked hat, braid and sword he cuts an impressive if incongruous figure, and hastens off to meet his wife at the station. As he leaves, we see Stan, having finally cleaned up everything to perfection, preparing to light a cheery "welcome home" fire. The logs won't light, for they are imitations, the façade for a gas fire, and Laurel,

having soaked them in gasoline, is about to strike a match.

A fadeout to a title which informs us that time has passed. Hardy returns from the station. His eye is blackened, his cocked hat crushed, his heroic looking sword crumpled and bent. Sorrowfully, Hardy surveys himself, and with his white-gloved forefinger traces the damage done to the point on his sword. His wife has walked out on him, so it hardly matters when he sees Laurel sitting in the smoking shell of his house—now nothing more than a front door, and the brick outline of the foundations. Vigorously he strides through the front door, to fall through the weakened and burnt floorboards on the other side. Although one is hardly possible, Laurel attempts an explanation: he still doesn't know what happened, and his story tails off in an outburst of tears. But when he sees that Hardy is too defeated to react in rage, he brightens considerably. "Well, I think I'll be going," he says, "There's nothing else I can do." Hardy, sitting dejectedly on the floor of his now open-to-the-skies "home," rejects the obvious comment and merely replies: "Shut the door on your way out. I think I'd like to be alone." Laurel leaves, and as soon as the door closes behind him, a peal of thunder rings out. The heavens open, and a deluge begins. Hardy, in his sailor suit, soaked to the skin and too uncaring now even to make that appeal for audience sympathy, simply sits there, accepting the worst that the world can offer. All that remains is his dignity, as he fastidiously uses two fingers of one gloved hand to squeeze a raindrop from the other gloved hand.

Off to meet Mrs. Hardy, leaving the house in Laurel's charge.

121

Yet another uneven struggle with Walter Long.

Any Old Port

HAL ROACH—M-G-M, 1932. *Directed by James Horne. Two reels.*

With Laurel & Hardy, Jacqueline Wells (Julie Bishop), Walter Long.

Sailors on leave, Laurel & Hardy check in at a sleazy hotel where they find that a pretty chambermaid is about to be forced to marry the gross and lecherous owner of the hotel. They champion her cause, but in order to earn money to effect her deliverance, Laurel is forced to enter a boxing match. His opponent turns out to be the would-be bridegroom. By a fluke, Laurel does win the bout—but his efforts are in vain and totally unappreciated by the girl, whose boy friend has suddenly materialized to take her away from it all.

An unsubtle satire of the mood and central situation of Griffith's 1919 *Broken Blossoms,* with Walter Long, himself an old Griffith villain, in the equivalent of the Donald Crisp role, *Any Old Port* is a singularly disappointing Laurel & Hardy effort. Hardy has some excellent dialogue, especially in the sequence where he sells Laurel to a fight promoter, and from the advance money eats a hearty meal, denying any food to the starving Laurel because he is "in training." But the climactic fight is surprisingly dull and unfunny, especially so in comparison with the similar and hilarious sequence in Chaplin's *City Lights* of the previous year.

Cause . . . .

The Music Box

HAL ROACH—M-G-M, 1932. *Three reels. Directed by James Parrott.*
With Laurel & Hardy, Billy Gilbert, Charlie Hall.

Laurel & Hardy, in business with a horse and cart, are hired to transport a piano to an address which turns out to be on the top of a hill, reachable by a long flight of steps. The long arduous haul begins, with frequent interruptions which send the jangling piano careening down the steps to street level again, often with Mr. Hardy in tow. Late in the afternoon they reach the summit, only to be told that they *could* have come the easy way—by road. Dutifully, they retrace their steps, and bring the piano back the *right* way. There is nobody home, and the difficult task of hoisting the piano through a window and unpacking it inside the house is not accomplished without a great deal of mishaps and destruction of property. Finally the piano is all assembled. But the owner of the house is incensed, and insists that they have made a mistake. He hates and despises pianos, and to prove his point he hacks it to pieces with an axe—just as his wife arrives to explain that it was a surprise birthday present. Suddenly contrite, he forgives the boys for having wrecked his home, and signs the receipt that Ollie gives him. But their pen "backfires" and, covered with ink, he chases them from his home in a blind rage.

An Academy Award winner (as the best short subject of 1932) *The Music Box* is one of the richest and most rewarding of all the Laurel & Hardy films and one of the best edited. Despite the fast that a full three reels are devoted to one basic gag, there is a continual variety of action, and a small but steady flow of new characters to lend punctuation to the various episodes. In its cutting as well as in its visual

. . . and two of the effects.

concept, it is almost like a very light-hearted equivalent of the famous Odessa Steps sequence in Eisenstein's *Potemkin!* The piano itself jangling its muttered asides, is almost as much of a "star" as the two comedians, imbued with a personality which enables it to make decisions and to move of its own accord. Despite the length of time that the operation takes (approximately two-thirds of the film have elapsed before the top of the steps is reached), the actual footage devoted to the laborious upward hauls and the rapid downward plunges is not as extensive as appears. In between are Laurel & Hardy's inevitable encounters with blustery Billy Gilbert, a cop, and a nursemaid. Hardy chivalrously attempts to remove the piano from its precarious perch halfway up the steps so that the nursemaid can squeeze by with her baby carriage. But the piano is more than a match for him, and drags him headfirst down to the street again. The nurse howls derisively at his stupidity, and when Hardy understandably remonstrates, she slowly and deliberately removes his hat and smashes the baby's bottle over his head. Unwilling to see his friend thus mistreated, Stanley gives her a swift kick in the derriere. Complaining to the rather unfriendly cop on the beat that she has been kicked "right in the middle of my daily duty," she leaves the scene, while the cop and his nightstick pick up and continue the action.

Such scenes effectively break up what might have been the monotony of a one-track gag of frustration, and even during the haulage scenes, "outside" gags are introduced as cutaways. At one point a hat is thrown from top to bottom of the steps, bouncing gaily all the way down to come to rest in the street just seconds before a truck arrives from nowhere to squash it flat. (Such gags, carefully and deliberately using the whole area of the screen, are often ruined when the films are shown today on wide screens, with the top and bottom of the frame completely lopped off). When the top of the stairs is finally reached, the emphasis of the film shifts a little: it is now what will happen to Laurel & Hardy, rather than what will happen to the piano, that becomes our concern. Unaware that he has reached the last step, Hardy blithely retreats backwards up the steps to a lily pond, and plunges in, the piano on top of him. Still later, the gag is repeated and expanded when, with the piano finally hoisted into a window, he guides it down the stairs, backs out of a landing window, and once more falls into the waiting lily pond, the piano toppling after him seconds later. And in the house, the customary wreckage done to the fittings, the front of Hardy's shoe cleaved off by a badly aimed stroke from Laurel's axe, the piano can now be removed from its wooden packing. As the boards are pried loose, gallons of water pour out, flooding the rapidly deteriorating living room. Hardy, sidestepping the deluge, manages to stand on one of the boards from which huge pointed nails protrude—an extremely painful gag, which softens its cruelty almost immediately, however. The sole of Hardy's shoe is ripped off, and he delicately tries to wrap the gashed leather around his exposed toes, to achieve dignity if not comfort. Cleaning up the rubble, the boys decide that music might help them so they turn on the player piano. In one of those charming and seemingly off-the-cuff musical interludes that they performed on occasion, they clean up the room by semi-dancing to the jaunty strains of "Turkey in the Straw" and finally join hands for a graceful minuet. But the peaceful and satisfying conclusion to their mission is shattered by the arrival of the wrathful Billy Gilbert, who proceeds to destroy the piano—although he too comes under its spell briefly. Nearly a total wreck, the machine plays its own taps with a gradually faltering "Star-Spangled Banner," while the three men stand at respectful attention.

The Music Box was by far the best of all their three-reelers, and together with 1933's *Busy Bodies,* the last of their handful of genuinely great shorts.

The Chimp

HAL ROACH—M-G-M, 1932. *Three reels. Directed by James Parrott.*

With Laurel & Hardy, Billy Gilbert, James Finlayson, Tiny Sanford.

Working with a bankrupt circus, Laurel & Hardy are paid off in "assets"—Laurel gets the flea circus, Hardy a trained chimp. Since animals aren't allowed in their rented room, they have to use strategy to get the chimp in, and when she *is* in, she takes over the best bed—leaving Laurel & Hardy to use the bed in which the flea circus has taken up residence. Since both the chimp and the jealous landlord's wife are

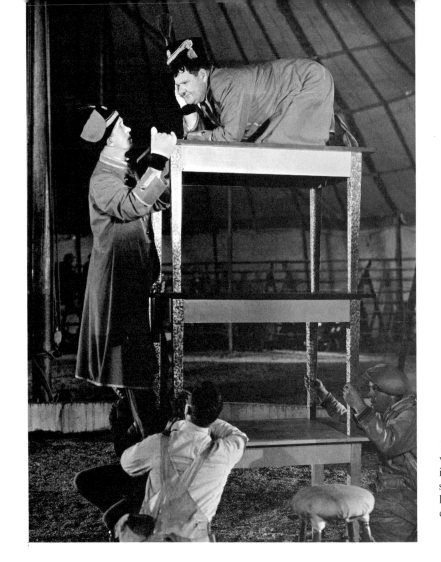

Laurel climbs to explain what went wrong with the cannon trick. Shot in closeup in the film, the empty spectator seats and the stagehands holding the tables in place were of course avoided by the camera.

Once more portly Ollie is minus his trousers.

126

named Ethel, the landlord suspects the worst when he hears Hardy repeatedly pleading with "Ethel" to come back to bed. He breaks in, gun ready, to accuse "the mother of my children," much to the consternation of Hardy and the real Ethel, who arrives just as the chimp seizes the revolver and begins to blaze away indiscriminately.

A relatively unknown and somewhat underrated comedy, *The Chimp,* a second partial remake of *Angora Love,* is just too thin to be stretched over three reels. The comparative slowness of the later sections is emphasized by the speed of the opening sequences in the circus, where Laurel & Hardy wreck the table-balancing and human cannonball acts so proudly introduced by ringmaster Finlayson. By-play involving the attempted crating up of Ethel (it winds up with her sealing Hardy into the crate!) and of a lion running loose through the streets are amusing;

the escaped flea circus is an episode that automatically sets one to scratching; and the highlight is undoubtedly Ethel's donning of a ballet skirt and prancing gracefully around the bedroom. Billy Gilbert, playing the jealous husband, was at this point in his career a specialist in loud and rather unpleasant character roles; minus his moustache for the most part, he seemed to be used as a kind of alternate for Richard Cramer in roles calling for blusterers and tough guys, but not outright villains. There was little humor in his work at this stage, and he became a far more appealing and inventive comedian in later years when he adopted a bushy moustache and wide-eyed confusion (as in *His Girl Friday* and Laurel & Hardy's later feature, *Blockheads).*

Although *The Chimp* disappoints, it is still a much better film than its relative obscurity would indicate, and is one of those curious comedies that never fails to come to life with an audience, getting louder and longer laughs than its slight material really warrants.

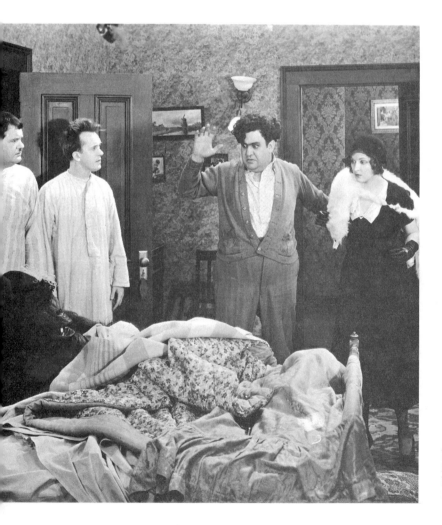

Billy Gilbert is relieved to find it isn't *his* wife in bed — but concerned by the violation of his "No Pets" ruling.

County Hospital

HAL ROACH—M-G-M, 1932. *Two reels. Directed by James Parrott.*
With Laurel & Hardy, Billy Gilbert.

Ollie, in hospital recuperating from an accident, is visited by Stan, who proceeds, quite unintentionally, to wreak more havoc on Mr. Hardy's person than the accident that placed him there and to engulf the unfortunate doctor (Billy Gilbert) in the resulting mayhem so that Hardy, cured or not, is discharged on the spot. Before leaving, Laurel accidentally sits on a hypodermic guaranteed to make him "sleep for a week" and in a semi-daze, drives Hardy home. A second accident is inevitable.

The first half of *County Hospital* is fine, vigorous, harmlessly sadistic stuff, with Hardy thoroughly trussed up in a hospital bed, his foot dangling from a pulley, and Laurel bringing him some hard-boiled eggs and nuts to cheer him up! Stan soon arouses the ire of Dr. Gilbert by calling him "Ma'am" by mistake, and we're into a typically violent slapstick sequence in which Gilbert is projected out of the window and saves his life by clinging to the pulleys of Hardy's traction, causing the unfortunate Ollie to be hoisted upside down by his injured leg. There's some amusing pantomime, too, in the efforts to dress Ollie, and pull his pants on *over* the gigantic bandages encasing his foot. "Cut the leg off!" explains Ollie patiently, referring of course to his trousers, while the anxious-to-oblige Stan takes a pair of scissors to Ollie's leg! But once outside the hospital, inspiration flags. The long latter section of the film is devoted to a wild ride through the busy Los Angeles streets, Hardy terrified, Stan—the driver—barely awake, thanks to the drug he has unwittingly absorbed. Unfortunately, except for a few brief cutaways, the entire sequence is sluggishly paced and edited, and staged entirely in the studio, with the most obvious and unconvincing use of back projection effects. With all of the escapes and near-collisions so patently phoney, there are neither laughs nor thrills in this very dull windup.

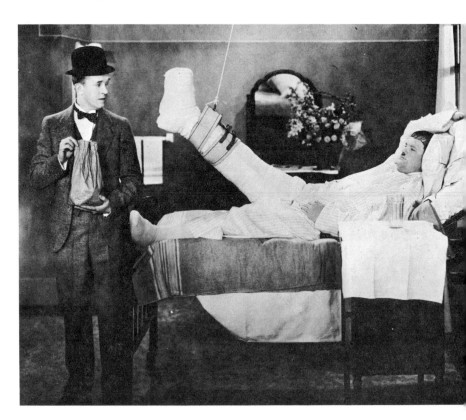

Hard-boiled eggs and nuts for Mr. Hardy.

Genial drunk Arthur Housman lets his buddies into the wrong house by mistake.

Scram

HAL ROACH—M-G-M, 1932. *Two reels. Directed by Raymond McCarey.*

With Laurel & Hardy, Arthur Housman, Richard Cramer.

Genial drunk Arthur Housman takes pity on the boys when he finds them in a torrential downpour, under orders from the local judge to leave town immediately or face a jail term as vagrants. He invites them to spend the night with him, but in his drunken state inadvertently takes them to the judge's house rather than his own. The judge arrives home just in time to find them in an entirely innocent, but very compromising, situation with his wife.

The lady of the house, Vivien Oakland, is in a playful mood.

Laurel & Hardy re-use their "laughter" gag.

With more subtlety than most of their recent films, but somehow with less fun, *Scram* doesn't entirely come off, and its director, Raymond McCarey, seems rather ill at ease with the comedians. Nevertheless, it contains at least two first-class episodes—their initial encounter with the drunk, who engages in small talk with them as they try to retrieve a coin that has fallen into a grating, all this in the midst of a driving rainstorm; and the climactic episode wherein Laurel, Hardy, and the judge's mildly inebriated wife collapse on her bed in spasms of wildly uncontrollable laughter.

Richard Cramer, the movies' foremost sourpuss (when not playing western heavies) is not amused.

Pack Up Your Troubles

HAL ROACH—M-G-M, 1932. *Seven reels. Directed by George Marshall and Raymond McCarey. Scenario by H. M. Walker. Camera: Art Lloyd.*

With Laurel & Hardy, Donald Dillaway, Mary Carr, Charles Middleton, Dick Cramer, Tom Kennedy, Billy Gilbert, Grady Sutton, Jacquie Lyn, James Finlayson, Richard Tucker, George Marshall.

It is World War I, and shortly before he is killed in action, Laurel & Hardy promise their best pal that they'll look after his little girl, and restore her to his wealthy parents. Back in America after the war, they try to keep their promise, but since they know only that his name was Smith, finding the girl's grandparents isn't an easy job, and orphanage officials are constantly on their heels to seize the child.

Made in 1931, but held back until late 1932 for its release, this second Laurel & Hardy starring feature was better constructed than the first *(Pardon Us)* but far less amusing. Most comedy teams, from Wallace Beery and Raymond Hatton to Abbott & Costello and Martin & Lewis, have found the Army comedy a fairly safe vehicle with which to establish themselves early in their career. And had Laurel & Hardy stuck to the service-life knockabout—far less overworked in 1932 than it would be a decade later—the formula might well have worked for them too. Certainly the funniest sequences appear at the beginning of the film, with George Marshall (the director) proving an apt comedian as a tough Army cook, and James Finlayson going through his usual paces as a short-tempered officer into whose quarters Laurel & Hardy empty all the garbage pails! But with the introduction of the little girl, plot and sentiment interfere far too often, and the film veers more in the direction of Jackie Coogan's *My Boy* than towards showcase sequences for Laurel & Hardy humor. As the mean official from the orphanage, Charles Middleton had some fine moments, but most of the strong supporting cast of character comedians was badly wasted.

Charles Middleton, orphanage meanie, warns them to give up the child they're harboring.

Their First Mistake

HAL ROACH—M-G-M, 1932. *Two reels. Directed by George Marshall.*
With Laurel & Hardy, Mae Busch, Billy Gilbert.

After one of the customary rows between Mr. and Mrs. Hardy, Stan suggests that a baby in the home might produce the desired harmony, and goes out to adopt one. Returning with the infant however, Hardy finds that his wife has left him. Moreover, she is suing him for divorce and Laurel for the alienation of her husband's affections. Morosely, Stan and Ollie tackle the job of feeding their new charge and getting him to sleep.

A classic in its way despite a meandering and inconclusive final third, *Their First Mistake* is one of the best and most original Laurel & Hardy comedies. The opening scenes of short-lived domestic bliss are superb. Laurel wants Hardy to sneak out with him for the evening: "I've got tickets for the Cement-Workers' Bazaar; they're giving away a steam-shovel." Ollie manages to persuade his wife that it's a big business banquet which will provide him with valuable contacts and chances for advancement. His hands floridly punctuating and emphasizing his words, he wins her over easily, darting frequent looks of guilt at the audience as she swallows lie after lie. Just as the scheme is working flawlessly, Stan phones

"What you need is a baby in your house."

and glibly spills the beans to Mrs. Hardy, who immediately gathers her weapons of war—saucepans, rolling pins, etc.—and unleashes her fury on her hapless mate. Stan arrives to witness the carnage, and when it is all over asks Ollie: "What did she say? Can you go?" Ollie wearily tells Stan, "She says I think more of you than I do of her," and, not unreasonably, Stan replies "Well, you *do,* don't you?"

Like two small boys who have been told they cannot go out to play, they retire to the bedroom, and in a beautifully conceived and executed sequence, literally retreat into childhood. They stretch out on the bed, and in frustration, boredom, and for the lack of anything else to do, shift positions, contort their limbs and try to change their "prison" into a kind of game—but boredom is still the end result. Then, while Laurel is propped on his back, feet in the air, one shoe being polished by a drape, an idea comes to

him. "What you need in your house is a baby!" he says emphatically. Hardy is intrigued, and Laurel, in one of his rare moments of inspiration and lucidity, goes on to explain that a baby will give Mrs. Hardy something to think about and keep her occupied, so that she could have no objection at all to her husband going out at nights with Laurel. Impressed, Hardy replies with the expected: "Tell me that again!" Laurel of course is unable to collect the thoughts of a moment ago, and the idea re-emerges as a disorganized garble. But the message has sunk in, and duly impressed, Hardy takes Laurel with him and they go out and in typically simplified movie fashion, return shortly thereafter with an adopted baby. But their careful plan falls apart at the seams: Mrs. Hardy has left for good, to sue for divorce. The hilarious sequence that follows is another reshaping of the betrayed-maiden satire that Laurel delivered so suc-

Director George Marshall plays a bit as a neighbor who congratulates the new "parents."

133

Night feeding problems: Laurel considerately opens the door for Hardy' moments after he has hurtled through it.

cessfully in *Putting Pants on Philip,* except that here it is Hardy who plays the victim, Laurel the betrayer, in dialogue and pantomime that beautifully spoofs the time-honored central situation of *Way Down East* and other melodramas of that ilk. Laurel wants to leave, but Hardy protests: "It was you that wanted me to *have* the baby and now that I'm in this terrible trouble, you want to leave me flat!" Laurel is sympathetic, but firm: "I don't want to get involved in this; I have my *future* to think of; my career!" By now Hardy is almost in tears: "You should have thought of that before we had the baby!"

It is largely Hardy's subtle facial expressions of despair and helplessness, coupled of course with the deliberately cliché dialogue, that makes the sequence work so well, and it is not surprising that the latter part of the film hardly lives up to three such excellent opening episodes. Problems of feeding, washing and pacifying the frequently crying baby allow plenty of opportunities for good sight gags, and they make the most of them. A rubber nipple on a hard-to-

handle baby bottle; Hardy's falls and tumbles as he seeks to minister—quietly—to the baby's needs in the middle of the night; the old gag of Laurel offering to feed the baby and methodically sitting down to unbutton his shirt (of course to take the bottle therefrom); and Laurel's own withdrawal into infantilism when it is *he* who falls asleep while sucking on the baby's bottle; all of this material is amusing and sometimes far more than that. But despite the comedy framework, Laurel & Hardy's comedy was usually close to recognizable reality, and the humor here is lessened by one's concern for a baby left in such incompetent hands. Furthermore, the sequence starts too late in the film for it to have time to develop story sense or a climax; thus it becomes no more than a series of funny gags which never resolve the situation, and the film merely comes to a rather unsatisfying halt on another gag rather than a conclusion. Nevertheless, despite the weaknesses of its last half, *Their First Mistake* must certainly rank as one of the best Laurel & Hardy comedies.

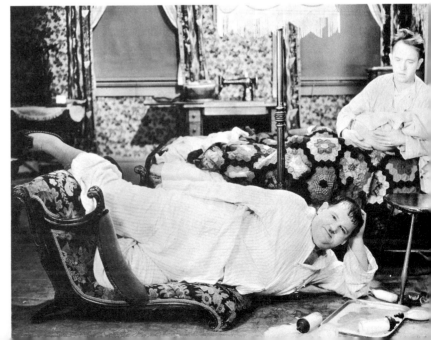

The light is on now; seconds ago it wasn't, hence Hardy's collision with the chair!

Towed in a Hole

HAL ROACH—M-G-M, 1933. *Two reels. Directed by George Marshall.*
   With Laurel & Hardy, Billy Gilbert.

Plying their trade as fish-peddlers, Hardy musically singing out "Fresh fish!" while Laurel blows on a horn, their old jalopy rumbling through the unresponsive Hollywood streets, the pair realize that their commercial future is bleak. Then Laurel has an idea: they'll buy their own boat, catch their own fish, elimi-nate the middle man, and keep all the profits. The next step, which also proves to be the last of this particular enterprise, is to buy an old boat and "fix it up."

One of their most diverting milkings of a single gag, *Towed in a Hole* concerns itself almost exclusively with the hammer and nails, saw and paintbrush brand of visual humor. The best gags are those of *antici-pation:* Hardy perched precariously atop the boat's mast to paint it, and hearing Laurel sawing below—

his face registering alarm, reassurance, and last-minute horror before the mast, skilfully sawn in two by Laurel, comes plunging down to land Hardy in a tub of whitewash. It is virtually a two-man show, Billy Gilbert's "role" as the seller of the boat being nothing more than an expository bit, and it is also a notably subtle film in its use of suggestion and sound to elevate all the gags from the level of mere slapstick. There is comparatively little dialogue, and indeed at one point, outraged by Laurel's stupidity, Hardy majestically states "I have *nothing* to say!" and maintains an even more marked silence. At the conclusion (the boat is being repaired on dry land, miles from the ocean) the boys put the boat on wheels and hoist a sail to facilitate its journey to the sea, whereupon a breeze immediately springs up and the now spick-and-span boat sails away, to destroy itself within seconds.

136

Twice Two

HAL ROACH—M-G-M, 1933. *Two reels. Directed by James Parrott.*

In dual roles, Laurel & Hardy play themselves and each other's wives, gathering for a special anniversary dinner.

The last moments of Hardy's pants — and his roses.

In the Laurel household, it is the wife who holds the purse strings.

One of their most original in concept but unfortunately one of their weakest in execution and comedy content, *Twice Two* is a misfire attempt to repeat the formula of *Brats*. There are some genuinely funny moments at the beginning: Hardy's agitated attempts to leave his office in time for the dinner, Laurel neatly decapitating a bouquet of Hardy's flowers by closing a door on them; but thereafter, despite the engaging pantomime of Laurel & Hardy as wives, and the four-cornered marital bickering, it soon bogs down into rather tiresome and repetitious gags.

Ollie gallantly helps his wife on with her wrap.

Mrs. Laurel inevitably meets the same kind of disasters as Mr. Hardy when being "helped" by Stanley.

Me and My Pal

HAL ROACH—M-G-M, 1933. *Two reels. Directed by Charles Rogers and Lloyd French.*
  With Laurel & Hardy, James Finlayson.

Newly-rich executive Oliver Hardy is about to secure his future by marrying the boss's daughter. While the bride and the wedding party wait with increasing impatience at the church, best man Stan arrives at Ollie's house to collect him, first making the mistake of giving him a giant-size jigsaw puzzle as a wedding present. Contemptuous of such a childish gift, Hardy nevertheless plays with it until the cab arrives—and soon cab-driver, policeman, butler, Western Union messenger and the boys themselves are busily engaged in putting it together. Finally the irate father arrives to announce the cancellation of the wedding, and the nearly-completed jigsaw is scattered to the winds in the furious melee that follows. Afterwards, Laurel laboriously starts to assemble it again, while Hardy's already upset marital plans are shattered by a telegram which tells him that his whole fortune has been wiped out by the stock market.

A curious essay in prolonged frustration, *Me and My Pal* is never quite as funny as it seems it should be, yet manages to be constantly amusing and even off-beat. Particularly enjoyable is the opening sequence in which Hardy listens to a radio interview with Laurel, nodding his head in thoughtful and modest approval as he, Hardy, is lauded as a genius. The bizarre interview comes to an odd conclusion when Laurel expresses his belief that the motion picture industry is still in its infancy!

Fra Diavolo (The Devil's Brother)

HAL ROACH—M-G-M, 1933. *Nine reels. Directed by Hal Roach and Charles Rogers. Script by Jeannie MacPherson. Camera: Art Lloyd, Hap Depew.*

With Laurel & Hardy, Dennis King, Thelma Todd, Lucille Brown, James Finlayson, Henry Armetta, Lane Chandler, Wilfrid Lucas, James C. Morton.

A burlesque of the famous operetta by Auber. The bandit Fra Diavolo poses as the Marquis de San Marco and in this guise gains the confidence of a flirtatious young lady and her rich and crotchety husband. Stanilo and Olivero, two wandering vagrants, decide to turn hold-up artists, but their first victim is Fra Diavolo himself. First ordering them to hang each other, he relents and takes them on as his servants and aides in a plot to relieve the married couple of their riches. Stanilo is not the most efficient of undercover men, and he inadvertently exposes his master's true identity. All three are stood up before a firing squad, but Stanilo makes up for his previous mistakes by accidently waving a red handkerchief.

A convenient bull charges the execution party, and the three bandits make their escape.

The first, and in many ways the best, of Laurel & Hardy's operatic lampoons, *Fra Diavolo* was both slicker, funnier, and more elaborate than their other features to date, and a much more entertaining foray into operetta than *Rogue Song* had been. The script, by DeMille's old reliable Jeannie MacPherson, treated the original plot-line and certainly the musical interludes in a reasonably straight fashion; thus the reversions to typical contemporary Laurel & Hardy routines, with the comedians hampered not at all by their period costumes, were doubly funny. Their material dominated and carried the plot-line, and was not merely there for comedy "relief" as in the earlier operatic venture. Too, the musical element was handled superbly by Dennis King, while as the flirty wife Thelma Todd was perfectly in the light opera tradition, so that those scenes in which Laurel & Hardy were off screen were genuinely entertaining and not merely buffers between comic highlights.

140

Reviews in 1933 were almost universally enthusiastic. "Everything that Laurel & Hardy have done in the past pales into insignificance in comparison with the comedy they introduce into this operatic extravaganza. Never have they put such enthusiasm into their work, and never have the gags flowed in such rapid and devastating fashion" wrote one critic, and added, "In his fooling Stan Laurel shows talent hitherto unsuspected, even, it might be whispered, to the extent of revealing the limitations of his teammate." Despite the deserved praise the film received, it should be remembered that most critics were aware only of the Laurel & Hardy *features;* the convictions that it was by far their best work, and that Laurel outshone Hardy, would probably have been less dogmatic had the critics as a whole been more familiar with the bulk of their work, which of course until this time consisted primarily of shorts. Nevertheless, *Fra Diavolo* was and is a most entertaining frolic, with its delightful music, romantic flavor and top-flight Laurel & Hardy routines. Laurel's attempts to hang Hardy at Fra Diavolo's orders, their protracted goodbyes, and finally the collapse of the tree under Hardy's weight, comprise an early comic highlight. Even better is one of those little vignettes of frustration that they did so well, in this case a game called "Earsie-kneesie-nosie" in which Laurel slaps his ears, nose and knees in a ritual pattern of perfect precision. Naturally, anything *he* can do Hardy can do better—until he tries, and has to give up in abject failure. The frustration is shared by the equally unsuccessful Henry Armetta and, one might add, by

Thelma Todd and Dennis King.

The best of Laurel & Hardy's numerous "laughing" routines.

141

The prelude to a piece of lively slapstick in which Hardy sways back and forth like a pendulum in reverse.

many members of the audience. It was something of a status symbol (although they didn't call it that in 1933) to be able to co-ordinate the earsie-kneesie-nosie movements successfully, and the game caught on like wildfire on park benches and in school playgrounds. Laurel's ability to do simple tricks with his fingers (a complex head-scratching routine was another *Fra Diavolo* delight)—tricks which confound Hardy, or boomerang unexpectedly—was a running gag in this film, and in many of their later features too.

Unquestionably, though, the funniest single gag in *Fra Diavolo* was a repeat of one of their best routines. Hopelessly drunk from sampling all the wares in the wine cellar, they collapse in helpless laughter. Everything that happens, including their own arrest and threatened execution, merely spurs an even greater laugh reaction. From giggles to chuckles and then to belly laughs, the sequence builds, grows and feeds on itself, relying not on incident but only on the infectious quality of laughter itself. Such a sequence, for maximum effect, demands a large and cooperative audience, and in 1933 the film certainly got such audiences, yet even on television this classic sequence still retains its remarkable comic persuasion.

The Midnight Patrol

HAL ROACH—M-G-M, 1933. *Two reels. Directed by Lloyd French.*
   With Laurel & Hardy, Charles Rogers.

Laurel & Hardy are conscientious but inept radio patrol policemen. After apologizing to a safecracker for interrupting his work while they phone headquarters, they find that the wheels have been stolen from their car. Directed to investigate a prowler, they are unaware that the miscreant is actually the Police Chief himself, accidentally locked out of his own home. Ultimately, and with much noise and commotion, they gain entrance, capture and knock out the "prowler" and return in triumph with their prize to the police station. When the chief regains consciousness, he is unimpressed by Hardy's tie-

Interested supervision of a safe-cracker at work.

143

Their efforts to force an entrance are crowned with success, if not with stealth and silence.

twiddling apologies, and as they are marched off screen, he borrows a revolver and metes out retribution. The rest of the force stand with heads bowed as they witness the execution of their comrades!

Almost a throwback to their 1930 days with its rather over-methodical pacing, *The Midnight Patrol* lacks the stiffness and awkwardness of those early talkies, however, and builds steadily to the spectacularly violent slapstick of their final entry into the house amid splintering doors, collapsing floors and barrels of flour and pickles. Slapstick is, for the most part, held in check and the bulk of the film veers to situational and dialogue humor.

Their initial encounter with the safecracker is a well-developed episode, and when they finally do see the light and arrest him, there is a further amusing sequence in which they try to find a day "convenient"

for him to appear in court, and wind up sacrificing their own days off in order to appear with him. There is also an unexpectedly uninhibited chunk of homosexual humor in their encounter with the tire thief. The business of breaking into the house is highlighted by a fine episode in which Laurel & Hardy use a heavy stone bench as a battering ram. Stepping backwards in order to gain momentum for their charge, Hardy topples into a deep lily pond, pulling the stone bench in with him. "Why don't you do something to *help* me?" he gurgles and bubbles from the bottom of the pool, pinned there by the bench, a predicament that we are shown in an overhead shot, as Laurel stands by in interested confusion. A lesser but very amusing Laurel & Hardy, *The Midnight Patrol* parallels Chaplin's *Easy Street* in that it presents the comedians ostensibly on the side of law and order, instead of fleeing from it.

144

Busy Bodies

HAL ROACH—M-G-M, 1933. *Two reels. Directed by Lloyd French.*
   With Laurel & Hardy, Tiny Sanford, Charlie Hall.

Laurel & Hardy are workmen in a woodworking shop.

Busy Bodies, one of the team's best sound comedies, and easily the best of their Lloyd French-directed films, literally has no plot at all. It has a *beginning,* with the boys happy in their work and at peace with the world, and it has an *ending,* wherein they are fired and, as a last straw, their car cut neatly in two by a huge saw; but the events that take them from point A to point B can hardly be considered to comprise a story. Virtually silent, other than for the shrewd use of sound effects, it concerns itself almost solely with violent and painful slapstick sequences which more than make up in vigor and eloquent pantomime what they lack in subtlety. The opening is disarming in its charm and simplicity: on their way to work, revelling in their good fortune at having solid jobs, and enjoying the bracing fresh air and sunshine, they decide that music would fit in with their happy mood. Stan pulls a cord in their car, and music appears—albeit one of the stock Hal Roach comedy themes! When it has run its course, they stop the car, lift the hood, remove the record from the ancient phonograph that does duty as a car radio, and, another record grinding out another Hal Roach theme, continue happily on their way. The day's work at the plant doesn't begin too promisingly however; Hardy is repeatedly knocked off his feet by workmen carrying planks of wood back and forth, and it isn't long before they're involved in a mildly fistic argument with Charlie Hall. But with work to do, Laurel doesn't permit the luxury of a prolonged set-to in their classic tradition. Ingratiating himself with Charlie, he offers him a cigar, lights it for him, and motions to him to sit down and puff at his ease. Audiences are of course waiting for the explosion, but the payoff is somewhat different: Laurel motions to the burly foreman (Tiny Sanford), points to the smoking Charlie Hall, and then to a prominent "No Smoking" sign. Hall is dragged away, his fate indicated by a dreadful off-screen commotion that suggests that he has, at the very least, been propelled headfirst into a greenhouse.

Minor distractions out of the way, Laurel & Hardy

Foreman Tiny Sanford is advised that Charlie Hall is smoking.

settle down to the day's work. It is never made quite clear what their duties are, for they never get beyond the careful scrutiny of pieces of wood, and the trying out of hammers, planes, and other tools of their trade. As Hardy thoughtlessly leans over the workbench, Laurel planes a huge strip from the ample rear of his trousers—and considerately pastes it back on with glue, an operation which Hardy's patient expression tells us is both futile and singularly uncomfortable. A further attempt on Laurel's part to help his friend merely results in Ollie's fingers being trapped in a window-frame—from which predicament Stan duly rescues him, but not without a fantastic contortion of Hardy's own frame.

Enough is enough, and work is put aside while the boys settle their personal differences in the usual sportsmanlike manner. Hardy gets very much the worst of the encounter, as doors, circular saws, and the contents of a closet (largely paint-pots of course!) descend on his head with resounding thuds, bangs, and clunks. The final offensive by Stan consists of taking a paintbrush, slowly and carefully soaking it in glue before the apprehensive but unflinching gaze of Mr. Hardy, and then ramming it home on the Hardy chin. But this ends the game: things have gone too far, and mere discomfort has become definite inconvenience. The paintbrush stays there, like a carefully nurtured beard, glued far too tightly to be re-

moved by hand. Instantly Stan is contrite and, all antagonism gone, wants only to help his pal. Tuggings and yankings being to no avail, Stan leads Ollie of the workbench, clamps the brush handle in a vise, and heaves. The handle comes off, but Hardy is left with a magnificently bushy beard. Scissors remove some of the unwelcome adornment, and Mr. Hardy's tie too—which Laurel helpfully drapes over Ollie's overalls, a sheepish grin seeming to say that it looks better that way.

In helping Ollie to loosen a tight window frame, Stan has trapped him in it.

146

The aftermath of one of Stanley's rare outbursts of temper.

Clearly, desperate measures are called for. Ollie is seated, draped with a towel as in the best barber shops, and his face lathered with soap. From his bag of tools, Laurel delicately selects a plane, which he hones on a grindstone. Just before he begins the shaving operation, he tests the sharpness of the blade against his fingernail, a resounding "ping!" assuring him of its efficiency. To the delicately blended sound effects of trees being uprooted and glass being scraped over sandpaper, Laurel pushes the plane over Hardy's jowls. Another "ping!" from the blade. Then an energetic sweep across Hardy's throat. Finally, grasping Hardy by the nose, Laurel puts the finishing touches to his shave with a horizontal dash across his mouth! The barbering over and the beard removed, Hardy fingers his tender chin and throat, amazed to find that it is all still there. And as Laurel hoses him down, Hardy assumes it's time for a little more retaliation. He yanks on the hose—and pulls the entire sink out of the wall. With unerring accuracy, it sails across the room to hit Hardy and send him floundering into the carpentry mechanism. Hoisted on belts, thrust through the floor boards, sucked into an air-vent, "spanked" by a mechanical paddle, Hardy finally reappears in a small outlet high in the outer wall of the plant. Laurel rushes to the rescue with a ladder, mainly to restore his friend's dignity by replacing his lost bowler. But as Laurel reaches the top of the ladder, Hardy suddenly becomes unstuck—and the pair of them plummet downwards.

Seeking escape, Charlie Hall falls face down in a tub of whitewash, while Tiny Sanford finds refuge in a tool shed seconds before the pair descend on it, reducing it to kindling. Sitting sorrowfully in the rubble, the boys are mystified by an urgent knocking at a door. It is repeated, and they suddenly realize that it is coming from the *other* side of the door on which they are sitting. They open the door—and there, literally crushed, is the foreman, whose expression leaves no doubt that their services are terminated as of that moment. Sadly, they pick up their belongings and leave. But, not quite recovered from their recent disasters, they are unmindful of the direction they are taking, and as they drive through a shed, a giant saw cuts neatly through their car, from front to stern. The car topples sideways into two useless halves. Not *quite* useless perhaps; Stan pulls the "radio" string, and the music starts up instantly. Beaming happily at this discovery that all is not lost, he turns to Ollie, who hardly shares his joy. Hardy chases Laurel off screen, pursued by a giant buzz-saw which optically wipes the scene into the "End" title. Despite its reliance on violent knockabout, *Busy Bodies* is a gem of a a comedy and one of their best. The timing is superb, only one or two gags being slightly prolonged beyond their basic worth, and the admittedly sadistic comedy routines have surprising variety, some being deliberately underplayed while others are exaggerated to equally deliberate excess.

147

Dirty Work

HAL ROACH—M-G-M, 1933. *Two reels. Directed by Lloyd French.*
    With Laurel & Hardy, Lucien Littlefield.

Lucien Littlefield is a genially crazy scientist, on the verge of perfecting a rejuvenation formula. Chimney sweeps Laurel & Hardy come to call just as he is successfully completing his twenty years of research by transforming a duck back into an egg. Calling the boys from their work to witness his triumph, he leaves them alone with his formula for a moment while he goes to find his butler, who will be his first human experiment. The boys, dubious, decide to experiment on their own by putting a fish into the vat of water. But Hardy, poised on the brink with a vial of the professor's formula, is knocked into it by the helpful Laurel. Only Hardy's terrified cries can be heard above the thrashing, boiling water. When the tumult dies down, the success of the formula is beyond question. Out climbs a chimpanzee, wearing Hardy's bowler hat. In reply to Laurel's

Hardy waits patiently for the last brick to fall.

tearful apologies, the chimp, with Hardy's voice, tells him contemptuously, "I have *nothing* to say."

An odd blend of traditional sight gags and science-fiction spoof, *Dirty Work* is a well-above-average Laurel & Hardy, with some genuinely funny dialogue both from the comedians and from the scientist's long-suffering and somewhat bemused butler. But although it is the rejuvenation gimmick that gives the film its story and substance, it is the less off-beat chimney sweeping scenes that provide the biggest laughs. "We've come to sweep your chimneys," chortles Hardy to the butler, his pudgy finger emphasizing the rhythm of his words, while the bored butler gives him decidedly peculiar instructions on how to find both the roof and the fireplace ("You can't miss the fireplace—it's standing against the wall!"). In no time at all, the luxurious living room is a soot-carpeted

shambles, and trying to shovel the soot into a bag that Hardy is holding merely results in Laurel's hacking holes in the carpet with his spade. Hardy, rambling into some delicious chatter as he discourses on a painting hanging on the wall, loosens his grip on the bag and holds out the generously ample tops of his trousers instead, while Laurel, equally absent-mindedly, continues to load the soot into this new receptacle. But the most elaborate and longest sustained gag concerns Laurel's attempts to shoot the long brush up the chimney to Hardy, waiting on the roof, a sequence that obviously has its roots in the aerial-construction of their earlier *Hog Wild*. Needing an extra extension, Laurel looks about the room, sees a shotgun of the right length, and attaches that. Up goes the brush—with an explosion that brings a duck, caught on the wing, hurtling down the chimney. Exasperated, Hardy yanks on the brush—and up comes a battered, dirty Laurel. A push, and down

Scientist Lucien Littlefield proudly announces his discovery.

he tumbles again into the by now filthy living room. *His* fighting spirit aroused, Laurel yanks on the brush too, and *down* comes Hardy. However, his girth prevents him from making the full descent. He is stuck somewhere just above the fireplace. Helpfully, Laurel reaches up, grabs his feet, and yanks. This time Hardy comes *all* the way down, with a sudden, sickening thud, followed by a shower of soot and bricks. Clouds of black soot billow outward, and as they settle, Hardy still sits there, waiting the final indignities. Two or three more bricks follow, slowly, deliberately, as though dropped by some unseen human agency, each one landing with a hollow thud on the same increasingly tender spot on Mr. Hardy's head. He waits. The deluge is over. With a sigh of relief, he looks curiously up the chimney. One final brick drops, selecting one of the few areas of Ollie's head hitherto untouched. And so it goes: a heavy clock falls from the mantelpiece onto Hardy's toes, its chimes settling up a discordant jangle that ceases only when Laurel "murders" the clock by bludgeon-

ing it to death with his shovel; on the roof, Hardy is alternately blackened by the unexpected thrusts of Laurel's brush, or washed white as snow when he is thrown headfirst into the greenhouse and thoroughly doused by the sprinkler system.

Dirty Work is more slick and mechanical than inspired, but it's a thoroughly amusing comedy nonetheless. It was also one of the last, if not *the* last, American comedies to use chimney sweeping as a stock comedy prop along with paperhanging and house-building. With the increasing use of central heating, the very idea of chimney sweeping began to smack of the Dickensian era, and in fact Hollywood films of the late 30's usually only admitted the existence of the sweep in a purely historical context (as, for example, in *Tower of London*). However, since chimney sweeping was, and still is, retained in Europe and especially in England, those countries continue to use occasional sweep comedy routines in their own slapstick films—though to far less amusing effect than in this Laurel & Hardy film.

Sons of the Desert

HAL ROACH–M-G-M, 1934. *Seven reels. Released in Europe as* FRATERNALLY YOURS. *Directed by William A. Seiter. Scenario by Frank Craven and Byron Morgan. Camera: Kenneth Peach.*

With Laurel & Hardy, Charlie Chase, Mae Busch, Dorothy Christie, Lucien Littlefield, John Elliott, John Merton.

Stan and Ollie are sworn to attend a fraternal convention, but the wives have other ideas. Pretending sickness, Oliver has a doctor order him on a long sea voyage, with Stan in attendance. The ruse works, and they are off to the convention. The very day that they return, however, word is received that "their" ship has been wrecked. Griefstricken, and to pass the time while waiting for news, the wives go to a movie—where they see a newsreel in which their husbands cavort gaily for cameras covering the convention. The boys, at home, discover the news of the shipwreck for themselves and manage to hide

Charlie Chase leads his fellow tent-members in some horseplay.

Home again, with ample proof of a Honolulu holiday.

in the attic just before the wives return home. Forced onto the roof and into the rain by the wives' exploration of the house, they finally "arrive" at the front door with a fantastic tale of their escape from a watery grave. Laurel breaks down under the stern eye of his spouse and confesses the truth, to be rewarded with luxury and comfort, while poor Ollie, who has tried to brazen it out to the end, feels the full fury of his wife's wrath.

Although a re-working of a theme that the comedians used quite frequently, *Sons of the Desert,* is a thoroughly fresh and delightful comedy, quite certainly the best and the subtlest of all their features. Straightforward slapstick is limited to a relatively few gags, and the humor derives principally from situations and characterizations. Flawlessly timed,

with ruthless (and profitable) pruning of the footage allotted to any one gag, the film is a particularly felicitous collaboration between Laurel & Hardy and director William A. Seiter, a specialist in romantic comedy and human drama. Unexpectedly, he turns out to have been the ideal director for them, polishing their own comedy values with his own wit, charm and taste. It is a great pity that this was to be his only film with them.

The material throughout is slight, but Seiter makes the most of every gag, without milking any of them. The solemn meeting of the Sons of the Desert, done in low-key lighting, serves as an admirable background for Laurel & Hardy's entrance. They are late, of course. They arrive shamefaced and embarrassed, miss each other at the door, stumble over assorted feet, and finally find empty seats, which they

With the news of the sinking of "their" ship, comes a night hiding in the attic . . .

152

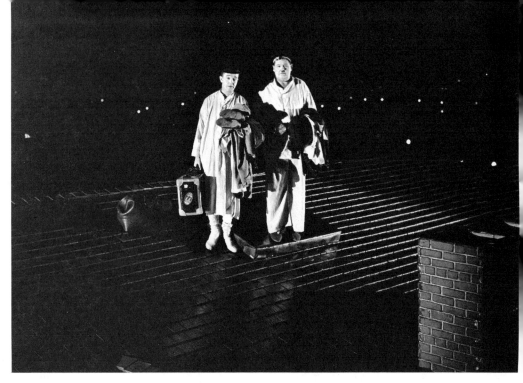

...and on the roof.

fill as hurriedly as possible, while the Exalted Ruler waits impatiently for the interruption to be over so that he can continue. Hardy smiles apologetically, and indicates that the speech should go on. But Laurel, shifting his chair sideways to be nearer his friend, crunches Oliver's fingers between the two chairs, and a mighty howl further interrupts the proceedings. Finally, all is serene, and the burnoosed Ruler goes on to explain the dread responsibilities of the Order. "The strong must help the weak!" he intones, while Oliver pointedly looks at Stanley in mute and rather proud acknowledgement of his own personal duty! For a while, the film maintains this rather gentle even keel—Hardy's broaching of the convention to his wife (Mae Busch); a vehement turndown; growing marital discord; and an odd sequence where Laurel determinedly chews away at some wax fruit. "So *you're* the one who's been eating all my fruit!" snorts Mae, catching him in the act and removing the rest of it from temptation!

The mood switches to furious slapstick temporarily, with Hardy's attempt to convince his wife that he is ill. With a simple prop—a metal tub full of hot water—a short, economical, yet riotously funny sequence is built. Initially, just Hardy's feet rest in the water, but in the course of a brief slapstick ballet, Mae is soaked by the hot water and Laurel's head is dunked into it beneath the weight of Hardy's body. The phony doctor called in to "diagnose" is a veterinarian, who proceeds to treat Hardy and to talk condescendingly to him as he would to a dog. The actual convention sequence is brief, yet riotously funny, with Charlie Chase scoring as an irrepressible practical joker, and a "Honolulu Baby" musical

Wives Mae Busch (left) and Dorothy Christie use their wiles to get Stan to confess.

153

Once more Hardy's chickens come home to roost.

number offering a devastating satire of crooner Dick Powell. And despite the sight gags inherent in the final third of the film—Laurel & Hardy trying to sleep quietly in hammocks in the attic; being caught in the rain in their nightshirts—it is dialogue that for once carries most of the comedy. Hardy's use of the phrase "like two peas in a pod," and his instruction to Laurel in the pronunciation of the word "pod," results in a running gag that is far better heard than described. Laurel is all for confessing the whole hoax, but Hardy, knowing the fate in store for *him,* will have none of it and threatens blackmail: "If you do, I'll tell *your* wife about the time I caught you smoking a cigarette!" Laurel is at first brazen, but then genuinely worried: "Would you *really* tell her *that?*"

The final showdown with the wives, in which the boys sink deeper and deeper into the morass of their own absurd story of escape (they came in ahead of the rescue boats by ship-hiking) is one of the funniest dialogue sequences they ever had.

Sons of the Desert has fewer virtuoso comedy episodes than such other major features as *Blockheads* and *Way Out West,* but thanks largely to Seiter's handling, it has that indefinable quality of charm which broadens its appeal quite beyond the legions of Laurel & Hardy devotees. Just as many of Seiter's films of the twenties, never considered either major works of art or important boxoffice contenders, prove to be amazingly durable today and of more value than many of their more highly regarded contemporaries, so I suspect in years to come will *Sons of the Desert* come to be regarded as one of the most accomplished comedies of the early 30's.

154

The Private Life

of Oliver the Eighth

HAL ROACH—M-G-M, 1934. *Three reels. Directed by Lloyd French.*
With Laurel & Hardy, Mae Busch.

Laurel and Hardy are struggling barbers, and Hardy sees a chance to improve their fortunes when he reads an advertisement by a rich widow who is seeking a husband. They present themselves at the lady's mansion and Hardy is accepted as the new husband. The prospects of immediate riches are soon replaced by concern however, for the butler is clearly mad—serving invisible meals to invisible guests—and it rapidly develops that the lady herself is mad, with a penchant for marrying men named Oliver and then murdering them. After a terrifying night, Oliver finally finds himself at her mercy, a knife at his throat—and awakens to find Laurel shaving him, the whole affair nothing more than a nightmare.

Their last three-reeler, with a title suggesting some kind of satire of the previous year's big success, *The Private Life of Henry the Eighth,* this film offered neither satire nor very much else that was genuinely funny. It is one of their slowest and emptiest films, the pantomime with the mad butler offering a few amusing moments, but most of the film falling back on stock "terror" jokes, including the old one in which Hardy shoots at a hand appearing over the bottom of the bed, the hand of course turning out to be his own foot. *The Private Life of Oliver the Eighth* was a surprisingly dull and banal film for a year in which their output was otherwise so consistently good. As in *The Laurel & Hardy Murder Case,* the dream ending was a distinct let-down.

155

Hollywood Party

M-G-M, 1934. *Seven reels. Directed by Richard Boleslawski. Screenplay by Howard Dietz and Arthur Kober. Music and lyrics by Rodgers & Hart, Arthur Freed, Gus Kahn, and others. Camera: James Wong Howe.*

With Laurel & Hardy, Jimmy Durante, Lupe Velez, Charles Butterworth, Eddie Quillan, Ted Healey, Polly Moran.

Musical comedy revue.

Generally conceded to be a disaster, *Hollywood Party* was released minus producer or director credits. Despite the top-heavy list of songwriters who worked on the film, M-G-M failed to back them up with worthwhile writing talent, and for an alleged "all-star" film, the cast was notably shy of any of the big-name M-G-M players. Laurel & Hardy, billed first, were certainly the most important names in the cast-roster, and yet their material had a casual, off-the-cuff look that suggested less thought and preparation than any minor routine in one of their shorts for Roach. Their silent, blow-burn, egg-breaking routine with Lupe Velez demonstrated once more that they could extract laughs from the slimmest of ideas and a minimum of props, but it was a curious waste of the finest talent in the film. It was later re-used in Robert Youngson's compilation film, M-G-M's *Big Parade of Laughs*.

Lupe Velez, who had been an extra in two of their silents, shared an egg-breaking routine with the boys.

Walter Long expresses displeasure at the boys' damaging testimony.

Ollie mimicks Stan's courtroom expression and question: "Aren't you going to hang him?"

Going Bye Bye

HAL ROACH—M-G-M, 1934. *Two reels. Directed by Charles Rogers.*
With Laurel & Hardy, Walter Long, Mae Busch.

Laurel & Hardy are key witnesses against killer Walter Long, who on their testimony is sentenced to life imprisonment. He swears to escape and wreak vengeance upon them, and when news of his escape reaches them, they decide to leave town in a hurry. Advertising for a travelling companion to share expenses, they catch Mae Busch, Long's girl friend. Unaware of their identity, she merely wants to leave town in a hurry because the police are on her trail When Long shows up too, she hides him in her trunk, which becomes locked. With axe, saw, and flaming torch, the boys helpfully try to effect his rescue, all unaware of the fate that awaits them when they succeed. The police finally arrive to recapture Long, but not before he has satisfied his thirst for revenge!

A casual reworking and re-arranging of several standard Laurel & Hardy themes, *Going Bye Bye* is a particularly slick, though never really distinguished, welding of violent slapstick and situational humor. The opening courtroom scene has some particularly amusing dialogue, with the judge first thanking the public-spirited Laurel & Hardy for their cooperation, and then sentencing Walter Long to life imprisonment. Indignantly, Laurel bounds to his feet: "Aren't you going to hang him?" he bleats. It is this, rather than his capture and sentencing, misfortunes that he has accepted as part of the game, that prompts Long's desire for revenge. Outside, in their car, Hardy mimicks Laurel's "Aren't you going to hang him?" and adds with real understatement, "Couldn't you see that he was *annoyed*?" Laurel's placing of the newspaper ad—a long, rambling, incoherent farrago—is another highlight, as is Hardy's ultra-gallant reception of Mae Busch as their cross-country travelling companion. As she outlines her sad tale of woe, climaxed by the improbable story of how her boy friend came to be locked in her trunk, Hardy's long stare at the audience reflects growing incredulity and disbelief, until his better nature, and his automatic pity for a lady in distress, asserts itself. "Sounds logical!" he murmurs to himself as the absurd yarn reaches its climax. The efforts to rescue Long from the trunk, in which he is rapidly suffocating, cause him to be almost impaled by screwdrivers, cut in half by a saw, suffocated by smoke (when they try to burn him out), drowned (as they pump in water to put out the fire!) and all but blown up. Finally released, his (off-screen) revenge consists of literally tying the boys in knots, with their feet tied decorously behind their necks. Climaxes of physical distortion such as this seemed to appeal to Laurel & Hardy's bizarre sense of humor, and in this film we last see them trussed up and seated on a couch, a scene that could have been taken from Tod Browning's *Freaks,* while Hardy intones the anticipated "Here's another nice mess you've gotten me into!"

Them Thar Hills

HAL ROACH—M-G-M, 1934. *Two reels. Directed by Charles Rogers.*

With Laurel & Hardy, Mae Busch, Charlie Hall, Billy Gilbert.

Gout-ridden Hardy, sent to the mountains to recuperate, is accompanied by his friend Mr. Laurel in a rented trailer. Camping out, they are delighted by the potency of the water they find in a well. "It's the iron in it," explains Hardy, not realizing that they have stumbled across the hastily jettisoned liquor of a band of bootleggers. Stranded motorists Charlie Hall and wife Mae Busch stop by, and while Charlie returns to his car with gasoline, Mae stays on to enjoy the kind hospitality offered by Laurel & Hardy. When Hall returns, he finds his wife hopelessly intoxicated from the well "water." Aspersions lead to insults, insults to violence. Within minutes, the peaceful camping site becomes a battlefield.

Apart from some traditional slapstick in the opening scenes—the typical "invalid" comedy of Laurel & Hardy, with the gout-afflicted foot being trodden on;

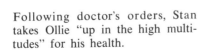
Following doctor's orders, Stan takes Ollie "up in the high multitudes" for his health.

Hardy, fully dressed, falling into the bathtub—*Them Thar Hills* is one of those slowly-paced, methodically building comedies in which the laughter comes as much from anticipation as from execution and climax. Finally out in the great outdoors, Laurel and Hardy are at peace with the world. Minor mishaps that in normal circumstances would precipitate quarrels are quickly forgotten. They'll relax, have fun, enjoy the recuperative powers of fresh air and sunshine. Their little caravan world is neat, tidy, orderly, running smoothly and efficiently. Quite obviously, it can only be a matter of time before the law of averages begins to work, and chaos descends. In the meantime, we too can relax and watch the fastidious Hardy as he elegantly prepares breakfast. "Coffee and beans!" he announces triumphantly, and Laurel, in a tone of genuine admiration, replies "Boy, you sure know how to plan a meal!" To be sure, there are minor altercations. Firewood is dropped on Hardy's painfully throbbing foot. The coffee and milk cans get switched, and Laurel's energetic work with the can openers results in a good deal of spilled milk. Not least, Laurel will insist on adding a climactic "pom-pom!" to punctuate a tune that Hardy is happily humming. Gradually becoming aware of the uncalled for accompaniment, Hardy firmly tells his friend, *"I'm singing this song!"* his humming taking on a new and menacing tone that just dares Laurel to interfere again. Of course, Laurel can't resist sneaking in one more "pom-pom"—and this time Hardy adds some punctuation of his own, using cooking utensils on Laurel's head.

But the good will generated by the water "with the iron in it" soon restores good fellowship, and the meal is progressing happily when Mr. and Mrs. Hall arrive. And when, having fixed his ailing auto, Hall returns much later, the happiness all around naturally arouses his suspicion. "You're drunk!" he snaps somewhat ungraciously at his wife and, his chivalry aroused, Mr. Hardy takes up the challenge. The warfare that follows is played according to the standard rules except that this time, being drunk, Laurel & Hardy have the bad manners to laugh uproariously at the misfortunes they heap on their opponent. These include cutting Hall's belt and placing a plate full of baked beans inside of his fallen trousers just seconds before he hoists them up again and dousing him with syrup prior to smothering him with feathers. Hall, stoically accepting all of this without a move in his own defense, naturally has his innings too, and, unhooking the trailer from the auto, makes an imme-

Preparations for their first breakfast in the great outdoors.

diate shambles of its interior. Finally he asks Hardy to bend down, and dubiously, curiously and obediently he does so. While Hall douses Hardy's trousers with gasoline, Hardy looks pleadingly at the audience—obviously he cannot be so ungentlemanly as to protest, but *surely* Hall can't be going to do what he thinks? Hall fumbles in his pockets. "Got a match?" he asks Stan. The obliging Stan does have a match. The match is lit and carefully applied to Hardy's backside. His trousers roar into flame, and he rushes around in confusion. "Jump into the well!" suggests Laurel; Hardy does so, and after a mighty explosion, his body hurtles skywards, to descend moments later with a mighty thud.

So savage—and so well received—was this encounter between Laurel & Hardy and their perennial enemy Charlie Hall, that for the first and only time in their career they planned a specific sequel. The follow-up film, *Tit for Tat,* was released the following year.

The end of a far from perfect day: Charles Hall hangs on to his dignity—and his trousers—while surveying the battlefield.

Babes In Toyland

HAL ROACH—M-G-M, 1934. *Nine reels. Reissued under the title* MARCH OF THE WOODEN SOLDIERS. *Directed by Gus Meins and Charles Rogers. Based on the operetta by Victor Herbert. Book and lyrics by Glen MacDonough. Screenplay by Nick Grinde and Frank Butler. Camera: Art Lloyd and Francis Corby.*

With Laurel & Hardy, Charlotte Henry, Harry Kleinbach (Henry Brandon), Felix Knight, Florence Roberts, Ferdinand Munier, William Burgess, Virginia Karnes, Johnny Downs, Marie Wilson, Jean Darling, Billy Bletcher, John George.

The nemesis of Toyland is the evil and lecherous Barnaby, who wishes to force innocent Bo-Beep to become his wife. It seems that he will succeed when he has her sweetheart banished to Bogeyland, and tries to take over Toyland with the armies of demons at his control. But the toymaker's assistants (Laurel & Hardy) who have constantly, if somewhat ineptly, opposed him, save the day when the giant-sized Wooden Soldiers, which they have produced by mistake, take command of all the other toys and defeat Barnaby's forces in battle.

Rarely seen in recent years (and not at all since the Walt Disney remake), *Babes in Toyland* is one of those unfortunate films that never seemed to turn up absolutely intact when revived in theatres or on television. TV considered some of the Bogey-Man footage too grim for juvenile viewing, and cut it accordingly. Earlier theatrical revivals often eliminated some of the charming songs, presumably on the theory that audiences were interested solely in Laurel & Hardy and that much of the rest of it was expendable. It is deplorable when any film is trimmed or slashed for revival showings, but it is particularly unfortunate here, for in many ways *Babes in Toyland,* in its original form, is the best of the Laurel & Hardy operettas.

Bo Peep (Charlotte Henry) and her two champions.

Certainly with its totally studio-created fantasy sets, it's the most elaborate. And in its emphasis on the musical element, it is the most satisfying in terms of the original work too. Laurel & Hardy fitted easily enough into *Fra Diavolo* and *The Bohemian Girl,* and musical and comic elements could be enjoyed equally well. But the dividing lines between those elements were quite clearly drawn; plot and music would stop for traditional Laurel & Hardy material, and then we'd be back in Bohemia again. Here, by the very nature of things, the boys are absorbed into the structure of the film and move along with it. This results in less material being specifically tailored for them than usual, but the end result is so pleasing that it is not altogether a bad thing. There is plenty of traditional Laurel & Hardy byplay, even if there are fewer slapstick tour-de-force sequences; and to the really devout Laurel & Hardy disciples, this byplay is usually more rewarding than the all-out slapstick routines. One of the funniest moments in *Babes in Toyland* comes when Barnaby thinks he has married a modestly

The evil Barnaby (Henry Brandon) menaces the young lovers.

Barnaby's bogey-men defeated by the Tin Soldiers, Laurel & Hardy, and a box of darts.

veiled Bo-Peep. After the ceremony, he finds that he has been tricked—he has actually married Laurel! Laurel's delight at his own cleverness quickly turns to dismay when Hardy tells him, "You'll have to stay *here*. You're married to Barnaby!" Between sobs, Laurel stammers, "But I don't *love* him!"

On all counts, this Hal Roach version is infinitely superior to Disney's gaudy, jazzed-up remake, which not only re-arranged and modernized the music, but rewrote the lyrics and added new songs as well. Here, apart from the briefest snatch of "The Cuckoos" in the main titles, and the use of Disney's "Three Little Pigs" theme, the music is all vintage Herbert, charmingly and faithfully rendered. Not *all* of the original music is utilized: "The Military Ball," "Barney O'Flynn," "Hail to Christmas," and "Beatrice Fairfax" are four casualties; but much of the omitted music appears in the form of incidental themes. For example, the original stage presentation featured a battle between a bear and a giant spider, and the music for this is used during the invasion of the Bogey-Men.

Disney obviously studied this version extremely

carefully before embarking on his remake. His two lead comics, for example, are so obviously patterned on the physical appearance and mannerisms of Laurel & Hardy, and so pathetically inadequate. But he came nowhere near matching the charm of this less pretentious version, and even his sadism (and cheerful, vigorous sadism has always been one of the most enjoyable aspects of Disney's work) didn't match the moments of genuine horror of the original. Roach's film was well served by its supporting players too. William Burgess as the toymaker was perhaps unremarkable, but he was certainly less offensive and imbecilic than Ed Wynn in the remake. Ray Bolger, a talented fellow admittedly, was never able to equal the superb villainy of Henry Brandon's Barnaby. (Brandon was then only in his early twenties.) As for Disney's Annette, she of course isn't in the same league as winsome and charming Charlotte Henry, the nearest the talkies ever came to a Betty Bronson. Worst of all, Disney had no authentic Victor Herbert—and no Laurel & Hardy. The 1934 *Babes in Toyland* has an enjoyably ample supply of both.

162

The Live Ghost

HAL ROACH–M-G-M, 1934. *Two reels. Directed by Charles Rogers.*

With Laurel & Hardy, Walter Long, Mae Busch, Charlie Hall, Arthur Housman, Leo Willis.

Workers in a fish canning plant, Laurel & Hardy enjoy their day off by fishing from a wharf. While thus engaged, they are approached by Walter Long, captain of a reputed ghost ship, who is having trouble rounding up a crew. At a dollar a head, they agree to shanghai a crew for him—which they do with remarkable success, only to wind up shanghaied themselves. The crew naturally wants to exact vengeance, but with the ferocious captain as protector for the pair, they have no opportunity aboard ship, and wisely Laurel & Hardy never leave the ship when it reaches port. Always enraged when the subject of the ghost is raised, Captain Long promises dire results

to any man who even mentions the word ghost: He'll twist his head so that when he's walking north he'll be looking south! Carefully, Laurel & Hardy contain their fears, but one night accidently fire off a revolver, and believe that they have killed their cabin mate. Actually, he's just dead drunk, as usual. To conceal their crime, they toss him overboard—but, revived by the water, he clambers back on board again—to fall into a vat of whitewash. The ghostly apparition causes panic among the crew, including Laurel & Hardy, who blurt out the fateful word "ghost" to the disbelieving captain. True to his word, he performs the neck-wringing operation, leaving them in "another fine mess!"

The plot of *The Live Ghost* is more than a little contrived, but it does allow for some exceptionally good individual sequences, while the settings of sleazy waterfront saloon and mist-shrouded ghost ship pro-

Disposing of the body of the sailor they have "killed."

vides opportunities for better and more carefully executed camerawork than was usual in their later shorts. The opening sequence contains some good, lively slapstick as Laurel & Hardy "recruit" their crew. Laurel goes into the saloon, bag of eggs in hand, and bets a likely-looking customer that he can't place the egg in his mouth without breaking it. The confident sucker carefully places the egg in his mouth, whereupon Laurel brings his fist up under the victim's jaw, and leads him a merry chase into the street outside, where Hardy is waiting with frying pan at the ready. The unconscious bodies are dumped unceremoniously into the hold of the ship—the long, pregnant pause between the actual dumping and the heavy thud as the body hits the floor indicating that it is a perilously deep hold indeed! Ultimately, for a change of pace, Hardy ventures into the saloon. His chosen victim is Charlie Hall, who unfortunately has witnessed Laurel's procedure. "Let me see *you* do it!" he suggests to Hardy, who innocently agrees—with the expected result!

The later scenes of Laurel & Hardy's apparent killing of their pal and their attempts to dispose of the body border on the morbid, although the situation is redeemed by some genuinely funny lines. In response to Laurel's plaintive question, "Do you think he's gone to heaven?" Hardy replies sadly: "I'm afraid not—probably the other place." Then he asks Laurel to find a chunk of coal (to weight the body). Laurel is indignant at this seeming breach of celestial etiquette: "Do you have to take your own coal when you go to the other place?" There is also an excellently timed, if familiar, sequence when the "dead" man returns to the ship as a white apparition. He slips into bed with Hardy, who fondly imagines that he is giving Laurel a stern lecture on the idiocy of giving in to the belief in ghosts. Raising his head to punctuate a point, he sees Laurel blandly staring at him from the other side of the port hole, lies down again, does a double-take, and sits up to find the "ghost" by his side, staring him in the face! Mae Busch, appearing briefly in the climactic episode as a waterfront floozie, has often been totally eliminated from the TV versions.

Tit for Tat

Charlie Hall defends his honor with two spoons of potato salad.

HAL ROACH—M-G-M, 1935. *Two reels. Directed by Charles Rogers.*
With Laurel & Hardy, Mae Busch, Charlie Hall.

It is opening day for Laurel & Hardy's brand new electrical appliances store, and thinking to exchange good will—and mutual free advertising—they call on the neighboring delicatessen store. Alas, its proprietors are Mr. and Mrs. Hall, whom they met so disastrously on their camping trip. Mrs. Hall wants to be friendly and cooperative. Hardy, beaming and spouting platitudes, suggests, "Why not let bygones be bygones—you help *our* business, and we'll help *your* business." But Mr. Hall wishes neither to forgive nor forget: "You mind *your* business and I'll mind *my* business!" Hardy withdraws with dignity, but moments later, atop a ladder to adjust some light bulbs, he is accidentally propelled into Mrs. Hall's bedroom. Seeing them walk down the stairs arm in arm, Hardy all gallantry, hand-kissing, and courteous small-talk, enrages Hall beyond all hopes of reasonable mediation. The war is on, starting in a small way and building to a crescendo, until every possible indignity has been inflicted on all three antagonists, and both the electrical and delicatessen businesses are denuded of wares.

For a film that is, in a sense, the definitive Laurel & Hardy sound film, and the equivalent of their silent classic *Big Business, Tit for Tat* is slightly disappointing. In terms of sheer laugh content, it must rank as one of their best, but it lacks subtlety and this time the orgy of ritual destruction does not arise naturally out of the action. It is clear from the outset that this is to be a "destruction" essay, and the boys get down to business as soon as possible, giving us a marvelous array of gags—quite as many as the varied products on hand in electrical and delicatessen stores would suggest—but little of the careful build-up or the joys of anticipation. Since the film is a sequel to *Them Thar Hills,* it can be argued, I suppose, that the earlier film was the "build-up" and this one the climax. Certainly the films fit logically and smoothly together to form forty minutes of explosive slapstick, although in point of fact the films were never shown that way theatrically, and it has only been in recent years that they have been shown in tandem by imaginative film societies.

The civilized and systematic exploration of the props in each store as machines for destruction results in some beautifully bizarre gags. Hall removes Hardy's bowler hat, and slices the brim from it on his humming bacon-slicing machine. He returns the violated hat to Hardy, who stares forlornly through the now hollow brim at the audience. Pats of potato salad are catapulted on to Hall's forehead, and the bottom drawer of his cash register is used to deliver a near knock-out blow to his chin. Having won their round, Laurel & Hardy return to their store, and Hall follows, looking around eagerly for the instrument that can quickest serve his needs. He finds his weapon in a pair of electrical pliers, plugs them in to a socket, applies the pincers to Mr. Hardy's nose, and watches in grim satisfaction as the smoke rises from the tortured nose! Delicately prodding and investigating his injured member, Hardy returns the foray

to Hall's store, and so it goes, back and forth, with Laurel & Hardy generally winning the day in terms of the infliction of personal discomfort, while Hall has a considerable lead in the destruction of valuable property. Hall is dumped in a crate of eggs, a huge cannister of lard is dumped on his head, and syrup is poured all over the money in his cash register. On the other hand, he hits back by gathering all of the watches in Hardy's store, placing them in a malted-milk container, and "mixing" them into a pile of rubble. Laurel, inspecting the debris, discovers a little wheel which can spin like a top, plays with it for a moment, throws it back with the rest of the junk, reconsiders, and contentedly pockets his new toy.

All this violent feuding naturally dominates the footage to such an extent that the film automatically works as a very funny comedy, but supporting and cutaway jokes tend to misfire. A running gag of a customer making off with Laurel & Hardy's merchandise without paying has him first walking out with a single vase and a polite "How d'you do?," then wheeling items out in a wheelbarrow, and finally loading appliances directly into a large truck. It provides punctuation, but just isn't as funny as it could be. The old gag of the marshmallows dusted with a sour powder, causing everyone to talk through pursed lips, likewise doesn't pay off. And the cop, anxious to make peace but not really of any help in stopping the carnage, is a pale shadow of Tiny Sanford's cop in *Big Business.* Nevertheless, *Tit for Tat* is a generally successful and often wildly funny comedy, certainly the last top-rank two-reeler that they were to make.

Bobby Dunn provides a running gag as the "customer" who systematically denudes Laurel & Hardy's store.

The Fixer Uppers

HAL ROACH—M-G-M, 1935. *Two reels. Directed by Charles Rogers.*

With Laurel & Hardy. Mae Busch, Charles Middleton, Arthur Housman.

Greeting-card salesmen Laurel & Hardy meet an unresponsive customer in Mae Busch and sympathetically listen to her tale of woe—an artist husband so much wrapped up in his work that he neglects her. Reluctantly, Hardy agrees to pose as her lover in order to make the husband jealous. The scheme works too well, and the furious husband challenges Hardy to a duel. The fateful encounter will not take place until the following dawn, and Hardy of course has no intention of keeping the appointment. But he and Laurel get drunk in a bar, and a friendly cabby, searching Hardy's pockets and finding the artist's card, takes Hardy "home" to that address. Finding the pair asleep in his wife's bed, the artists prepares for the duel there and then, but Mae puts blanks in her husband's gun and tells Hardy to play dead. The scheme works, until the still unappeased husband announces that he is going to cut the body into little pieces. Hardy comes back to life in a hurry, and he and Laurel beat a hasty retreat, with the jealous husband in hot pursuit.

A simplified and funnier remake of one of their earliest silents, *Slipping Wives,* this is a generally amusing film completely dominated by Hardy. His initial encounter with Mae Busch is a joy, first reading with great gusto and feeling examples of the asinine greetings cards that he and Laurel have composed—one of them being his "Four-in-One Special" that takes in Christmas, New Year's, Easter and the Fourth of July. When he senses that something is wrong, he tries, with great tenderness, to wring the secret of Mae's troubles from her. "Did you lose your job?" interjects Laurel abruptly, rudely shattering the sympathetic mood that Hardy has nurtured. A later gem of a sequence has Hardy fatalistically anticipating the next dawn's duel, until Laurel reminds him that the artist has no idea *who* he is, and that all he has to do is not show up. Hardy's joyful realization that all that stands between him and death is honor rapidly turns to anger at Laurel for not having told him this before, and then to sudden courage. He calls the artist on the telephone: "If you think *I'm* going to waste *my* time to fight a duel with *you,* you're crazy!"

But the highlight of the whole film, and indeed one of the funniest scenes that the comedians ever did, is a long, beautifully paced and edited sequence in which Mae shows Oliver how a lover should kiss her by practising on Laurel. She grabs the stiff and unresponsive Laurel in a tight close-shot of their two heads, whispers seductively to him, and presses her lips to his. Laurel still doesn't react, but the camera frequently cuts away to Hardy's face, capturing its alternating expressions of disbelief, amazement, and impatience. In long-held shots, he shares his incredulity with the audience, beginning, after a while, to time the kiss with his watch; then listening to his watch to make sure that it is still going; assuring the audience that it is, and finally turning back to the still-kissing couple just before they break their clinch. Laurel falls swooning to the floor. But as Mae begins to explain to Hardy that *that's* how she should be kissed, Laurel, suddenly revived and very much aroused, bounces back and embraces Mae passionately, giving her another torrid kiss. When they break this time, it is Mae who faints!

167

Thicker Than Water

HAL ROACH—M-G-M, 1935. *Two reels. Directed by James Horne.*

With Laurel & Hardy, Daphne Pollard, James Finlayson.

After witnessing Hardy's humiliating encounters with his wife and the rent collector, boarder Laurel talks him into putting his foot down and showing that *he's* the boss of the household. Hardy—his wife fortunately out of earshot—agrees, and to prove his new-found manhood he draws their entire savings out of the bank in order to take over financial leadership in such mundane matters as rent, furniture payments, and so on. Passing an auction sale, they are enticed in—and chivalrously agree to help an old lady who is bidding on a grandfather clock, but who has insufficient capital to buy it. They'll keep the bidding open until she returns. Alas, the bidding closes before her return, and Hardy finds himself the unwilling possessor of an expensive clock which consumes *all* of the withdrawn savings. However, he is not its possessor for long. Crossing a busy street, they have to put their heavy burden down for a moment and it is immediately crushed to kindling by a passing truck.

Crestfallen, they get home moments before Mrs. Hardy, who by now has heard what happened at the bank. Hardy's attempts to appease her are in vain, and Laurel winces as he listens to the off-screen sounds of battle. When the dust settles, Hardy has to be rushed to the hospital for repairs. An immediate blood transfusion is necessary, and although Laurel tries to escape, he is trapped into being a "volunteer." But the doctor is nervous, and the equipment not in proper working order. Too much blood is taken from first one, then the other, pumped back and forth in an effort to restore the balance. After the operation, the two personalities have become inextricably confused. Laurel, wearing Hardy's clothes and moustache, pantomimes his pal's gestures and indignantly intones, "Here's *another* fine mess you've gotten me into!," while Hardy, minus moustache and dressed in Laurel's clothes, breaks down into helpless tears.

Thicker Than Water was Laurel & Hardy's last two-reeler, before moving exclusively to features, and it is a pity that it couldn't have been a more inspired farewell to the shorts field. While some scenes, and particularly a breakfast-table sequence between Mr. & Mrs. Hardy and boarder Laurel, were typical and up to their best standards, the film as a whole had a tired look to it, with some overlong and footage-consuming dialogue routines. It often happens, of course, that the last film in any series—when there are no hopes or plans for a renewed contract—is done quickly and cheaply, to finish off a commitment so that the decks can be cleared for something else. It is understandable in a way, since extra time and effort expended is not likely to bring in any extra revenue. *Thicker Than Water,* however, is not cheap or slipshod in its production; indeed, it employs some fancy and costly optical wipes between scenes which are quite creative in the way they move the story to its next location with both speed and humor. It is in its plot, its casual throwing together of tried and true situations, and in the sometimes unfunny dialogue stretches, that the lethargy shows. However, if it isn't the spectacular wrap-up to Laurel & Hardy's shorts that one would have liked, it is also far from being one of their really weak comedies. The last shorts made by Chaplin, Keaton and Lloyd were also far from being their best, quite possibly deliberately, in the knowledge that the feature to come would inevitably be compared, and perhaps to its detriment, with the shorts that it was replacing.

Bonnie Scotland

HAL ROACH—M-G-M, 1935. *Eight reels. Directed by James Horne. Scenario by Frank Butler and Jeff Moffitt. Camera: Art Lloyd, Walter Lundin.*

With Laurel & Hardy, June Lang, William Janney, David Torrence, James Finlayson, Anne Grey, Vernon Steel, Maurice Black, Daphne Pollard, Mary Gordon, Lionel Belmore.

Journeying from America to Scotland to collect an inheritance, Laurel & Hardy discover that all they have been left is an item of sentimental value—a snuff box. When their young Scottish friend joins the Army, a circumstance forced on him so that he will be unable to marry the girl he loves, Laurel & Hardy join up too. The regiment moves to India. The girl follows, but even in India the difference in their "stations in life," helped along by conspiring relatives, serves to keep them apart. But when the young man, with the help of Laurel & Hardy, puts down a native uprising, all misunderstandings are swept away and he and his sweetheart are finally united.

A sad disappointment for the initial entry in the comedians' features-only policy, *Bonnie Scotland* was to remain one of their weakest features, though its lessons seem to have been taken to heart. Far too much footage was devoted to the incredibly old-fashioned romantic sub-plot, which was not even played with the tongue-in-cheek derision it deserved. The hero (William Janney) was such an unappetizing weak sister that the heroine's remarkable devotion to him was hard to accept. Production values were sur-

prisingly shoddy, with cheap sets, uninteresting locations, and many stock shots. Finally, the element of spectacular action (even if comic action) so essential to this type of film, a lampoon of the *Lives of a*

Stan just having asked the constable where to find a policeman, Ollie explains that his friend is new to Scotland.

Sergeant James Finlayson has once again come off second best.

Bengal Lancer school, was totally lacking. The film started off well enough, with an appealing and convincing Scottish village set (undoubtedly borrowed from a contemporary M-G-M production) and an enjoyable concentration on Laurel & Hardy. Their initial encounters with Scottish citizenry and customs, their disappointment at the reading of the will, and an amusing sequence in which they try to broil a fish in their hotel room (a candle providing the heat, the springs of their bed a grille) all seemed to bode well. But once the romantic sub-plot was introduced and the locale shifted to India, both imagination and production values went out of the window, and a slow-paced lethargy took over. True, there were enough Laurel & Hardy highlights to prevent boredom from setting in, but even the best moments lacked zip, or were repetitions of previous gags. Their tiltings with James Finlayson were restrained, and a sequence in which they rhythmically clean up a courtyard to the accompaniment of the band's rehearsals of "A Hundred Pipers" is merely a prolonged and less effective reworking of their impromptu dance in *The Music Box*. Diminutive Daphne Pollard had some amusing moments as a firebrand of a Scotch lady's maid, exploding now and then with such pseudo-Scotch expressions as "Well, toss me over the 'urdles!," but there was much too little of her. The expected big slapstick finale fizzles out disappointingly when the boys upset beehives among the tribesmen. In fact, the film fades out to its "End" title in this sequence, without bothering to wrap up plot or bring in a neat closing gag.

Laurel & Hardy about to wear out their welcome at the palace of Maurice Black.

The Bohemian Girl

HAL ROACH—M-G-M, 1936. *Seven reels. Directed by James Horne and Charles Rogers. Scenario by Alfred Bunn, from the opera by William Balfe. Camera: Art Lloyd, Francis Corby.*

With Laurel & Hardy, Antonio Morena, Jacqueline Wells (Julie Bishop), Mae Busch, Darla Hood, William P. Carleton, James Finlayson, Zeffie Tilbury, Mitchell Lewis, Felix Knight, Lane Chandler, Paulette Goddard.

Based on the operetta by Balfe, this is a tale of gypsies who, offended by the master of a noble house, kidnap his only child, and raise her as one of their own. Years later, the gypsy band returns to the same

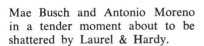
Mae Busch and Antonio Moreno in a tender moment about to be shattered by Laurel & Hardy.

James Finlayson obviously relishing the chance to flog gypsy girl Jacqueline Wells.

locality, where the old nobleman still mourns the loss of his daughter. The girl, now a young lady, in love and unaware of her past, is betrayed by a jealous gypsy woman and wrongly blaimed for a theft from her father's house. About to be flogged for the crime, her identity is unexpectedly revealed and she is reunited with both her father and her lover.

The last and weakest of Laurel & Hardy's operatic spoofs, *The Bohemian Girl* was nevertheless a very entertaining comedy, and a big improvement on *Bonnie Scotland*. Perhaps because of its old-fashioned plotting (even by operatic standards) it has never been made into a *serious* musical film, although a rather enjoyable silent version was made in England in 1922, with Ivor Novello, Gladys Cooper and C. Aubrey Smith. Curiously, the Laurel & Hardy version retained a surprising amount of the original's

straight plotting, contributing neither to the musical nor to the comedy aspects. Musically, "I Dreamt I Dwelled in Marble Halls" was rather over-plugged, while the other musical themes were merely suggested in the background scoring. The decision to remain reasonably faithful to the original work, while eliminating almost all of the music and not restoring the balance by an added stress on comedy, was an odd one, especially since the successful formula created by *Fra Diavolo* and *Babes in Toyland* hardly seemed to call for a new departure. Nevertheless, the film moved quickly, and Laurel & Hardy's routines, including another torture-chamber episode, were well up to standard. And as Bohemian gypsies, they were able to add yet another picturesque garb to the remarkably varied array of uniforms, costumes, and plumed hats that they wore in their movies.

172

Daphne Pollard, smallest but most aggressive of Hardy's screen wives, indulges in some back-seat driving.

Our Relations

STAN LAUREL PRODUCTIONS for Hal Roach—M-G-M, 1936. *Six reels. Directed by Harry Lachman. Screenplay by Richard Connell, Felix Adler, Charles Rogers, and Jack Jevne from the W. W. Jacobs story "The Money Box." Camera: Rudolph Maté.*

With Laurel & Hardy, Alan Hale, Sidney Toler, James Finlayson, Daphne Pollard, Iris Adrian, Noel Madison, Betty Healy, Lona Andre, Ralf Harolde, Arthur Housman.

Sailors Laurel & Hardy are entrusted with a package (containing a diamond ring) to deliver on shore. Aware of their own weaknesses, and determined that on this shore leave they won't fritter away their savings, they leave their money with their captain, making him promise not to return it to them under any condition until they have set sail again. The port into which they have been thrust is by coincidence the home town of their long-lost and now happily-married twin brothers. The sailors pick up two waterfront girls in a saloon, while not far away the civilians are

Captain James Finlayson insists that the boys remove their clothes so they'll stay put.

entertaining their wives in a slightly more respectable beer parlor. The inevitable soon takes place, and the twins become inter-mixed. The temporary loss of the diamond involves the boys with gangsters, and unable to produce the missing gem, they are encased in teetering cylinders of cement and left on the edge of the wharf for the law of gravity to take its course. None too logically, the tangled threads are straightened out at the last minute, marital suspicions dispelled, and the long separated twins reunited.

Produced by Stan Laurel's own company for Roach, and thus spared the occasional interference by Roach, whose changes in gags and plot structure often caused friction and dissatisfaction though never any serious rifts on a personal level, *Our Relations* was on a much bigger scale than any prior Laurel & Hardy film. The elaborate night club set in which much of the action took place was a really impressive creation, and the whole production has a look of class and polish to it. No little of this can be attributed to the smooth, glistening camerawork by Rudolph Maté, the only really creative cameraman that Laurel & Hardy had used since the departure of George Stevens many years earlier. Director Harry Lachman, who never worked with them before or since, was

But a rendezvous with Alan Hale *has* to be kept—and is.

174

Assorted nemeses Sidney Toler and Arthur Housman (left) and Ralf Harolde and Noel Madison (right) converge on the boys at a night club.

hardly a comedy specialist, but a versatile all-around craftsman (one of his more notable credits was *Dante's Inferno*) who seems to have left the comedy routines pretty much to Laurel & Hardy and to have devoted his efforts to keeping the tangled plot-lines fairly cohesive and to creating genuine menace and suspense in the climactic gangster episodes.

Based, though somewhat loosely, on a story by W. W. Jacobs (author of that Grand Guignol classic, "The Monkey's Paw"), *Our Relations* also has more than a casual relationship to Shakespeare's *Comedy of Errors,* or at least to the musical show made from it under the title of *The Boys from Syracuse*. More might have been made of differentiation between the sets of twins; other than the fact that the sailors are fun-loving and free and easy, and the husbands mildly henpecked, both Laurel & Hardys are identical in mannerisms and in their relationship with one another. However, the film moves too quickly and covers too much ground for there to be much time to ponder such a criticism. While slapstick is there in full measure, it is again comedy of frustra-tion that dominates: The sailors vainly trying to per-suade the captain to return their money, and being locked in their hotel room, sans clothes, "for their own good"; the husbands' attempts to convince their wives and beer parlor proprietor Alan Hale that they were *not* there earlier with two blonde pickups; and so on. The traditional encounter with James Finlay-son was even more savage than usual. With mustard plastered under his toupee, and an electric light bulb screwed into his mouth, he came off a decided second-best in this particular fray. The trick pho-tography when the twins finally meet was fairly elementary, even for 1936, but was smoothly and convincingly done by Maté. Slightly morbid at times, especially in the cement barrel sequences, *Our Rela-tions* is nevertheless one of the most handsome Laurel & Hardy films, and because of its production values, one that holds up best today. Television re-vivals have been especially ruthless to it in terms of cutting, however. There is even a *one*-reel version under the title of *Sailors' Downfall*.

175

Way Out West

STAN LAUREL PRODUCTIONS for Hal Roach—
M-G-M, 1937. *Six reels. Directed by James Horne.
Screenplay by Jack Jevne, Charles Rogers, James
Parrott, and Felix Adler. Camera: Art Lloyd, Walter
Lundin.*

*With Laurel & Hardy, Sharon Lynne, James Fin-
layson, Rosina Lawrence, Stanley Fields, Vivien
Oakland, Chill Wills, The Avalon Boys, Mary
Gordon.*

Laurel & Hardy come to Brushwood Gulch in the
Wild West to deliver the deed to a gold mine to the
daughter of a recently deceased partner of theirs.
Their enquiries of saloon owner James Finlayson
prompt him to palm off his brassy partner as the
heiress, and taken in by her, they hand over the deed.
Later they encounter the genuine heiress, employed
as a kitchenmaid in the saloon, and determine to get
the deed back. Their initial efforts get them run out
of town, but a final nocturnal foray into the saloon
crowns their efforts with success.

With the possible exception of *Sons of the Desert*,
which was subtler if not funnier, *Way Out West* must
rank as the best of all the Laurel & Hardy features.
Not only is it pure, unadulterated Laurel & Hardy,
with no time wasted on subsidiary plotting or romantic or musical "relief," but it is also a first-rate satire
of the Western genre. Most such satires have usually
consisted of putting a comic—Jack Benny, Bob Hope,
Martin and Lewis, Abbott & Costello—through their
customary paces against a Western backdrop, which
is often not exploited at all. The Marx Brothers came
closer to genuine satire with their *Go West,* and
Laurel & Hardy, though denied the budget the Marx
Brothers had and thus limited in their spoofing of
spectacular action sequences, succeed perhaps best of
all. Their characters are beautiful takeoffs on the
standard wandering cavaliers, while James Finlayson,
cast as Mickey Finn, outdoes himself as the epitome

Stan innocently tells all to scheming Mickey Finn (Finlayson) while Ollie registers annoyance.

of double-dyed villainy, the sheer joy of chicanery almost outweighing the monetary rewards it will bring. Finlayson's direct stares at the audience, often done in direct counterpoint to Hardy's (Hardy would appeal for sympathy, while Finlayson's stares were aggressive, as if *daring* the audience to do anything with its knowledge of his own perfidy) here are extended and exploited as never before. As he outlines some particularly heinous piece of villainy, he rubs his hands, chuckles, leaps for joy and looks to the audience for admiration of his cunning; or as he tells some exceptionally outrageous lie, he stares at the camera with an exaggerated intake of breath, over-awed himself by his own skulduggery.

There isn't a wasted moment in *Way Out West*. Even when the plot isn't being propelled forward, there are delightful little vignettes and the establishment of running gags. Early in the film, Laurel & Hardy, accompanied by their mule, wade through a river. Hardy's aplomb, and the position of the camera, tip us off to what is coming—and, sure enough, he steps into a hidden pot-hole, and plunges beneath the surface of the water. Familiarity was too much an essential part of the Laurel & Hardy format for it ever to breed contempt, and thus the gag works even better when it is repeated at the end of the film as a wrap-up, this time with the comedians walking *away* from the camera instead of towards it.

An amusing, but admittedly rather protracted, early sequence in which they are confused by a signpost which the wind keeps shifting into different directions was never included in the U.S. release version, but was retained in the European prints. (Laurel

& Hardy films, extremely popular in Britain and Europe, invariably played at the top of the bill, where the short running times were sometimes a handicap).

Hitchhiking a stagecoach ride into town, Hardy engages the lone lady in the coach in some marvelous small-talk. "A lot of weather we've been having lately," he begins coyly, and adds assininity to absurdity, the convivial gallant and the intruding bore all rolled into one, while his captive audience smiles politely, hoping he'll shut up. Hardy of course is merely seeking to bring a little old-world grace and charm to this wilderness, and he is rudely taken aback when they reach their destination. The lady is met by her husband, the burly sheriff, who asks if she had a nice journey. Yes, she tells him, except for that awful man who bothered her from the moment he got into the coach. The sheriff gives the boys until the *next* coach to get out of town. With the plot proper not yet under way, Laurel & Hardy still find time to dally outside the saloon, and go into an extemporaneous and charmingly executed soft-shoe shuffle. It is performed in one long take, like a vaudeville routine, with an audaciously obvious back projection screen (cowboys, horses, wagons going about their business in the dusty street) immediately behind them. An unexpected bonus later in the film is a second such musical interlude when, as punctuation between two comedy episodes, the boys relax in the saloon and sing "In The Blue Ridge Mountains of Virginia," performed simply and pleasingly, easing into comedy only for its climax, when Laurel is hit on the head and switches from a shrill falsetto to a deep base.

Clearly defined "good" girl and "bad" girl—Rosina Lawrence as the slavey, Sharon Lynne as the saloon girl.

The first encounter with the bogus heiress provides some superb comedy. Laurel & Hardy, too trusting and goodnatured to see through the sham sweetness and phony tears of the gold-digging impostor, are entirely taken in by her. Hardy has cautioned Stanley to break the sad news gently, but Stanley, unfamiliar with the ways of diplomacy, blurts out the news with a bald statement and seems pleased with his information. "Is my poor daddy really dead?" croons the bogus heiress tearfully, and Stan solaces her with, "I hope so—they buried him!" With dignity, Hardy rescues the delicate situation and hands over the deed to the mine. A family locket has to be handed over too, but this somehow has slipped into his shirt. Stan's efforts to help Ollie find it soon cause the pair

to be hopelessly enmeshed in a tangle of shirts, buttons, and suspenders, while Hardy, by now in a state of unseemly dishabille, murmurs his apologies to the presumably genteel young lady, who is doing her best to express polite shock, while Finlayson's face can express nothing more than ill-concealed impatience. Their mission finally completed, however, the boys leave, only to run smack into the genuine heiress. Now in possession of all the facts, they rush back to Finlayson's room and indignantly demand the return of the deed. Finlayson and his crony, now revealed in their true colors, refuse and a wild free-for-all develops, with the deed being passed from hand to hand, and thrown across the room, like a football. For a time, the deed is safely in Laurel's possession,

178

One of the highspots of the film:
The bedroom scene wherein Sharon
Lynne regains the deed.

but the scheming saloon girl, in a reversal of clichéd seduction scenes, chases Laurel into her bedroom, locks the door behind her, and throws herself on Laurel, who is cowering timidly on the bed. With the camera recording the titanic struggle from above, side and from under the bed, Laurel is finally defeated when the vamp resorts to tickling as a last measure, and immediately reduces him to a state of screaming hysterics. One of his funniest variations on their old laughing routine, it is one of the highlights of the picture. Rendered quite helpless by this onslaught, he is of no further use to Hardy—thereafter the girl has only to approach him and he collapses in hysterics again—and the deed, recovered by the villains, is locked away in their safe.

Another brief period of repose provides the opportunity to develop some of the running gags a little further. One of the best involves Laurel's ability to snap his fingers and turn his thumb into a flaming torch with which he lights his pipe. Hardy, despite strenuous efforts, is unable to duplicate the feat, and finally gives it up as not being worth the bother. Of course, he achieves success when he least expects it—

a casual flick of his fingers later in the film (during a nocturnal foray after the deed) turns his thumb into a veritable flaming beacon!

The longest single slapstick sequence is retained for the climax, when Stan and Ollie break into Finlayson's saloon at night. First comes the problem of climbing into the upstairs window, a problem solved—apparently—by a pulley system and a mule. As Hardy sails majestically upwards, Laurel tells him, "Wait a minute, I want to spit on my hands!" There is a moment's horrified realization for Ollie before he plummets downwards. Despite their attempts to be secretive, the howls of pain and ear-shattering sounds of collapse, collision, and destruction attendant on any Laurel & Hardy burglary venture, naturally arouse the nightshirted Finlayson from his slumbers. Racing up a ladder, Hardy is caught when the flap of a trapdoor falls squarely on, and over, his head, encircling it like a millstone. The door is jammed, and there is Hardy's head, emerging through the floorboards. Laurel grabs the head between both hands and yanks—and an elasticized replica of Hardy's head and neck is stretched some three or

Two western knights and the damsel they have championed head for a happy future—seconds before Ollie disappears into a hidden pothole!

four feet before boomeranging back to its original position with a resounding thud. Finlayson's footsteps are getting nearer, so Stan hides Ollie's head under a convenient tin pail and scampers away to conceal himself. Finlayson leaps into the attic with a triumphant bound and surveys the scene with wide eyes and wrinkled-up nose. As he crosses the room, he trips over the awkwardly placed pail. Annoyed, he aims a furious full-bodied kick at the offending implement. Thanks to Hardy's ample head being wedged inside, the pail refuses to budge, and Finlayson hobbles off, nursing his injured foot, while Laurel comes out of hiding to ease the pail off his pal's somewhat battered head. The final confrontation takes place when the boys take refuge inside a piano, the tinkling notes tipping off Finlayson that something is amiss. Stealthily looking inside the piano, he spots his prey, and nods a confirmation of his dis-

covery to the audience. Then he sits down and plays a lively jig, each dull thud on the keyboard telling him that he has hit home. Finally, the piano collapses in a jangling mass of wires and splintered wood, and the chase is on again, winding up with Finlayson first hoisted up to a chandelier and tied there by his nightshirt, and finally trapped in the steel shutters surrounding his saloon.

Way Out West is 100-proof undiluted Laurel & Hardy, and one of their best showcase vehicles. Even though it inevitably has certain echoes of previous films, it has no actual repetition of specific earlier gags, and is so crammed with incident that there is no time for those slowly-developed milkings of single gags which so often alienated non-partisans of Laurel & Hardy. Understandably, it was one of their best-liked features.

180

Pick a Star

HAL ROACH—M-G-M, 1937. *Eight reels. Produced and directed by Edward Sedgwick. Scenario by Richard Flournoy, Arthur Vernon Jones, and Thomas J. Dugan. Camera: Norbert Brodine.*

With Jack Haley, Patsy Kelly, Rosina Lawrence, Mischa Auer, Charles Halton, Lyda Roberti, Tom Dugan, Russell Hicks, Spencer Charters, Robert Gleckler, Joyce Compton, Sam Adams, Johnny Arthur, James Finlayson, Walter Long, Wesley Barry, Johnny Hyams, Leila McIntyre, Benny Burt, and Laurel & Hardy in guest roles playing themselves.

A typical Hollywood Cinderella tale, in which the young innocent (Rosina Lawrence) from the country achieves stardom with the help of a publicity man (Jack Haley).

In this unambitious, but extremely pleasant, film musical with a Hollywood background, Laurel & Hardy played themselves in two long sequences which totalled about a reel of footage. In one, Hardy swallows a tin whistle and Laurel gets tunes from it by poking Hardy in the stomach, an old gag but played here with finesse and imagination. The second sequence shows them filming a western saloon brawl with Walter Long as their antagonist, and afterwards demonstrating to studio visitors how all of the bottles, chairs, etc., are easily breakable lightweight props—until, in their over-confidence, they forget themselves and knock themselves out with the genuine articles. Riding the crest of their popularity at the time, they were often billed as the stars by exhibitors, which naturally caused some resentment against the film. This was a pity, for the film had a lot of charm and was generally quite superior to most of the non-Laurel & Hardy features that Roach produced. Rosina Lawrence, the heroine of *Way Out West,* and again here, was a Roach protégé with a pleasant manner, good looks, and an above-average singing voice. She never quite caught on, however, and disappeared from films soon afterwards. Despite their relatively limited footage, the Laurel & Hardy scenes were highlights of the production, and funny enough to please even those who were disappointed in not finding the film a starring vehicle for the comedians. In any case, there was a much more serious development for Laurel & Hardy admirers to worry about. Their contracts with Roach were drawing to a close, and both rumors and official publicity predicted that there would be only two more Laurel & Hardy films, after which the team would split up permanently.

Swiss Miss

HAL ROACH—M-G-M, 1938. *Seven reels. Directed by John G. Blystone. Scenario by James Parrott, Felix Adler, and Charles Nelson, from an original story by Jean Negulesco and Charles Rogers. Camera: Norbert Brodine.*

With Laurel & Hardy, Della Lind, Walter Woolf King, Eric Blore, Adia Kuznetzof, Charles Judels, Ludovico Tomarchio, Jean de Briac, George Sorel, Charles Gamore.

Laurel & Hardy are mousetrap salesmen touring Switzerland as the logical outlet for their product, since the country that produces Swiss cheese must surely also produce a proportionate number of mice. When one of their demonstrations in a ritzy hotel goes awry, they are put to work in the kitchen, where their mentor is a ferocious, knife-wielding cook. For every dish they break, he adds another day to their servitude, marking it on a blackboard. Their enforced stay coincides with a local music festival,

and they find themselves unwitting cupids in helping to patch up the tottering marriage of two temperamental singers.

Although in recent years *Swiss Miss* has attained an almost legendary status by virtue of critic James Agee's pithy and appetizing description of one single gag situation, it is, as a whole, a very disappointing film. Not since *Bonnie Scotland* had they been afflicted with a script containing so much padding, "relief" in the form of prolonged musical numbers, and unnecessary plot. The fact that the two opera singers were not conventional ingenues, and indeed were even unsympathetic and ridiculous at times, hardly compensated for all the footage devoted to

them. Too, one missed the familiar Roach faces, especially that of James Finlayson. Reputedly, Laurel had been ill before and during production, and he certainly looked wan and tired much of the time, as well as being so overweight that he appeared to be almost as heavy as Hardy. And allegedly, Roach interfered a great deal and insisted that certain gags be altered, completely killing the point of at least one routine, according to Laurel. However, even without such interference, it is unlikely that *Swiss Miss* could have overcome the obstacles of the script and the lethargic pacing. All of which is a great pity, for the film had a zany near-surrealism in many of its comedy sequences, more akin to the earlier work of the Marx Brothers and René Clair than to Laurel &

Walter Woolf King and Della Lind as the temperamental husband-and-wife singers.

Hardy's usual comfortable exaggeration of reality. There was a frenzied desperation to the kitchen sequences, Laurel dropping plate after plate, watching the chalk-marks on the blackboard multiply alarmingly, and surreptitiously trying to erase them.

Brilliantly conceived, though executed in a disappointingly flat fashion, was a sequence in which Laurel tries to seduce a steadfast St. Bernard rescue dog into giving up his supply of brandy, and finally succeeds by staging a fake snowstorm with chicken feathers and simulating the death-throes of a starved and frozen mountaineer. The sequence, perhaps suggested by a similar episode in a Disney cartoon,

Alpine Climbers, is capped by the dog's mournful realization of his dereliction of duty! The climactic episode, the one so beloved by James Agee, finds the boys moving a heavy piano up a narrow mountain trail and over a swaying trestle bridge—in the middle of which they encounter a gorilla! The scene reads rather better than it plays, for much of its punch is blunted by uninspired editing, too-static camerawork, and a complete lack of even superficial realism due to over-obvious back projection and painted backdrops. Moreover, the gorilla has such an endearingly human personality that it comes as rather a shock when he is finally heaved into the yawning chasm to

Ludovico Tomarchio, the terror of the kitchen, finally gets his come-uppance from his long-suffering helpers.

his death. Perhaps as an afterthought to this sequence, he reappears in the closing scene of the film, bandaged and on crutches, to chase the boys out of the scene and away from the interminable music that has taken over once again. Nevertheless, as the apparent next-to-last Laurel & Hardy vehicle, it was well received by both critics and audiences, who seemed charitably blind to its many flaws.

Transporting a piano across the Alps becomes, in Laurel & Hardy's hands, a feat comparable with Hannibal's famous march over the same route.

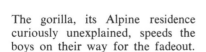

The gorilla, its Alpine residence curiously unexplained, speeds the boys on their way for the fadeout.

184

William Royle orders his men "over the top."

Blockheads

STAN LAUREL PRODUCTIONS for Hal Roach—M-G-M, 1938. *Five reels. Directed by John G. Blystone. Screenplay by James Parrott, Harry Langdon, Felix Adler, Charles Rogers, and Arnold Belgard. Camera: Art Lloyd.*

With Laurel & Hardy, Billy Gilbert, Patricia Ellis, James Finlayson, Minna Gombell, Harry Woods, Harry Stubbs, William Royle.

It is World War I, and the "Big Push" is on. Hardy goes over the top, and Laurel is left in charge of the trench. Twenty years go by, and unaware of the Armistice, Private Laurel sticks resolutely to his post, a mountain of empty bean cans mute testimony to the passage of time. Discovered by accident, he is taken back to America and fêted as a hero. Hardy, now married, reads the story and goes to claim his old pal, promising him a wonderful meal from a wonderful

Hardy promises to look after the long-lost pal who has apparently left a leg on the battlefields of France.

Out of touch with the mechanics of modern life for so long, Stan unwittingly dumps a load of sand on his friend . . .

wife, and a home until he is re-established. But Mrs. Hardy has had enough of the "bums" that her husband brings home, and after making it abundantly clear to Laurel that he is *not* welcome, she stalks out. In readjusting to civilian life, Laurel manages to wreck Hardy's car, his garage and his apartment, and innocently but inextricably gets himself and Ollie involved with a pajama-clad blonde from next door, just as *her* husband and Ollie's wife return. Stan and Ollie beat a hasty retreat to the blasts from a brace of shotguns.

Although it turned out not to be the last Laurel & Hardy as planned, *Blockheads* is the last vintage comedy that they made, the last in joint collaboration with Roach and M-G-M, and their last feature of real stature. Audiences in 1938 were honesly saddened by the thought that this would be the farewell film from the beloved comics. The critics, not affected so sentimentally, and still not convinced that Laurel & Hardy were comedians of major importance, were far from kind. Most thought the film quite weak, and some had the temerity to suggest that if this was the best Laurel & Hardy could do, then it was high time that they split up and went their separate ways. Of course, today, with the current paucity of good visual screen comedy, it's easy to accept that *Blockheads* seems much funnier than it did thirty years ago. Yet, at the same time, 1938 was hardly a year rich in comedy. The cycle of crazy comedies was spiralling

to a close with *It's Love I'm After* and *Merrily We Live*. Chaplin was between pictures; the Marx Brothers and Ernst Lubitsch were obviously slipping; Harold Lloyd's work was apparently at an end, and Buster Keaton was being wasted in cheap shorts. Laurel & Hardy were the last defenders of visual comedy, and snubbing a film as rich in inventive humor as *Blockheads* seems quite beyond comprehension. The very things criticized were the factors that made it such a delight. It had no "plot," but Laurel & Hardy had never needed plots, and their worst films were those with the most story. It was just a series of gags, as in their two-reelers. Well, pure concentrated Laurel & Hardy is surely an asset rather than a liability, and *Blockheads* is absolutely undistilled Laurel & Hardy, just as *Way Out West* had been. Almost like old vaudevillians before the final curtain, they trot out their old and proven routines, embellish others, and throw in a few new ones too. There are gags in *Blockheads* borrowed directly from *Helpmates, The Music Box, Unaccustomed As We Are,* and others. Former comedy star Harry Langdon, one of the writers, borrows too, and there are many traces of gags from his own silent comedies *The Strong Man* and *Soldier Man*. The many new gags range from subtlety to slapstick, and from pantomime to farce. One of the best of Laurel's running gags is his unique ability to pull down the *shadow* of a window shade. Again, the uncomprehending Hardy tries and tries again to find substance in Laurel's shadows, all to no avail. Until of course, the time that he tries it in an unguarded moment, and is rewarded by having the shadow of the window shade whoosh upwards at his touch with a resounding clatter.

One of the longest gags, attacked by some critics as being in bad taste, probably because truly black humor was rare and misunderstood in films of the late 30's, occurs when Ollie goes to collect Stan from the soldiers' home. Stan has been walking in the grounds and, tired, sits down in a wheel chair, one leg folded under him. It is thus that Hardy finds him—and assumes that his friend has lost a leg in the war. Overcome with compassion, too embarrassed to mention the affliction, Hardy insists on wheeling Stanley to the gates, thoughtfully rushing to get him a drink of water, and performing any other menial tasks that he can, even picking Stan up and carrying him to his car when the wheel chair is claimed.

Stan, his initial protestations unheeded, begins to enjoy this unusual pampering. Hardy at one point has to rest for a moment and, without thinking, puts Laurel down; thus when he is ready to resume his journey, Laurel jumps up again to be cradled in Ollie's arms. Suddenly, realization dawns on Ollie's face—and with it the awful understanding that Stan really hasn't changed so much in two decades. The determination to "do right" by his pal remains, but the old Laurel & Hardy relationship is quickly reestablished. Hardy needs parking space for his car,

and asks Laurel to please move the truck that is blocking the way a few yards farther up the street. Obligingly, Laurel hops into the cab of the truck, pulls a lever, and although the truck remains where it is, we hear the sound of hydraulic gears in action, and get a glimpse of the rear portion of the truck being elevated. Our next view of Hardy is of his head, neatly topping the mountain of sand that has been dumped from the truck to completely cover Oliver and his car. In rapid succession, Stan wrecks the auto and Ollie's garage, not understanding the mechanics of the automatic doors. The elevator being temporarily out of order, the boys are forced to trudge upstairs to their apartment. En route they encounter an obnoxious freckle-faced brat and, with some justification, kick his football downstairs—where it flattens both the desk clerk, and top-hatted businessman James Finlayson. But the brat has a tough father, who insists that the boys retrieve the football—and so is introduced another running gag, the periodic running up and down those long flights of stairs, a comic effect that is heightened by the trick set, a "shaved" in half apartment building which follows the stairway from top to bottom.

Even such a simple operation as opening a door isn't wasted. Hardy, key ring attached to his trousers, inserts the key in the lock, and Laurel helpfully turns the knob and opens the door. With a rending of fabric, Hardy is suddenly bereft of his pants, standing there in his underwear, plump thighs and knees ex-

. . . and moments later wrecks his car and garage.

Harry Woods in an altercation with a momentarily aggressive Laurel.

posed to the shocked gaze of his neighbors. Mrs. Hardy's viper-tongued harangue finally convinces Stan that he is not going to get the thick juicy steak promised by Ollie. But Ollie is a man of his word— a steak Stan has been promised and a steak Stan will get. Unfortunately this involves lighting the gas stove, a maneuver Ollie has never been able to manage without blowing up the kitchen. And so it goes. *Blockheads* admittedly has no plot, but one chaos dovetails neatly into the next. Hardy's meticulously laid plans and his domestic bliss are systematically shattered. Pomposity and politeness are reduced to screaming mayhem, and Stan, the unwitting cause of it all, sits patiently on the sidelines, quite unable to figure it all out. *Blockheads,* aided by the production polish that Stan Laurel always gave to those films that were his personal productions (and helped too, by some impressive footage from *The Big Parade* in its opening war sequences) maintains its marvelous pace until about five minutes from the end, by which

time it has involved itself in the basic plot-line of *Unaccustomed As We Are*—the next-door wife hidden in the trunk, the jealous husband and Ollie's wife forming a complicated triangle. Then, suddenly, it falls flat. Neither Laurel & Hardy, nor the writers, nor director John Blystone (who had directed Keaton's memorable *Our Hospitality)* seem to know how to wind it all up. Characteristically, they settle for a repeat of an old gag—the climactic joke from *We Faw Down,* in which a couple of shots fired from an apartment window send dozens of erring husbands scrambling from adjacent windows. Perhaps because there has been insufficient build-up, it doesn't work as well here as it did in the earlier film, which is a pity. One would have liked the last major Laurel & Hardy work to come to its conclusion with a triumphant smash. But in view of all the excellent material that has gone before, one can readily excuse this brief lapse.

188

1939

While continuing to release the Laurel & Hardy films through M-G-M, Hal Roach had, from 1937 on, used United Artists as the distribution outlet for his increasing activity in more ambitious features, ranging from comedies like *There Goes My Heart* and *Topper Takes a Trip* to actioners *(Captain Fury, One Million B.C.)* and his one outstanding dramatic film, *Of Mice and Men.* In 1939, with Hardy still under contract after Laurel's agreement had expired, Roach used him in one more film, *Zenobia* (retitled *Elephants Never Forget* in Europe), produced by Eddie Sutherland and directed by Gordon Douglas. Since Hardy was supported by Harry Langdon, there was some speculation that Roach might be trying to create a new comedy team. Although this was hardly likely, it was a good publicity gimmick and nothing was done to dispell it. A rather charming period romantic

comedy, it gave Hardy a comparatively straight role, rather in the Will Rogers manner, and proved once again that he *could* be an actor when given the chance. But audiences, not unnaturally expecting a continuation of the Laurel & Hardy brand of humor, were disappointed by the fact that Hardy was more subdued than usual, that he and Langdon were not really teamed in the accepted sense, and that Langdon's humor was far removed from Laurel's. Actually, for a comedian who was considered a has-been, Langdon made a remarkably smooth comeback and had some extremely funny footage. But the public had forgotten that he was once a serious rival to Chaplin himself and measured him only by the standards of Laurel. Even had Roach been thinking of a Hardy-Langdon series, it is improbable that such a team would have caught on.

The Flying Deuces

RKO RADIO, 1939. *Seven reels. Produced by Boris Morros. Directed by Edward Sutherland. Screenplay by Ralph Spence, Harry Langdon, Charles Rogers, and Alfred Schiller. Camera: Art Lloyd and Elmer Dyer (aerial photography).*

With Laurel & Hardy, Jean Parker, Reginald Gardiner, Charles Middleton, James Finlayson, Jean Del Val, Clem Wilenchick.

Oliver Hardy, jilted by the girl he loves and despondent, wants to commit suicide and plans to jump in the Seine. Stan is willing to help him leave this world, but is reluctant to accompany him. Fortunately, tragedy is averted when a Foreign Legionnaire talks them out of it, and persuades them to enlist in the Legion to forget. This proves rather difficult when his wife turns out to be the very girl who had jilted Hardy. The pair makes somewhat inefficient soldiers,

It's Paris, it's spring, and Ollie is in love with flirtatious Jean Parker.

When she turns him down, there's only one solution—but Stan finds it hard to understand why he must share Ollie's misfortunes.

and as a climax to their many misdeeds are sentenced to be shot at dawn. They make their escape in an airplane, but after a wild ride it crashes. Laurel escapes unhurt, but Hardy is killed—only to reappear almost instantly, reincarnated as a horse.

More than a year had elapsed since the release of *Blockheads,* and Laurel & Hardy devotees avidly awaited this re-teaming of their favorites. Despite a script concocted by their old cronies and the presence in the cast of such reliable comedy foils as Finlayson and Middleton, it just didn't jell and seemed to lack the old spontaneous cameraderie of the Roach films. Despite occasional good gags, it was mechanical stuff and seemed like *Beau Hunks* and *Bonnie Scotland* all over again. Highlights, of which there were too few, included Laurel's "playing" a prison bed spring like a harp, and a pleasing little soft-shoe shuffle. Good photography, especially in the aerial scenes, was the only tangible production asset. The film was cheaply made, with the RKO sound stages themselves thinly disguised to serve as "sets" for desert fort and plane hangar.

A new life in the Foreign Legion—and a cheerful little dance when they arrive.

Finlayson follows them from army to army, and here assigns them their cells, cheerfully reminding them that they are to be shot at dawn!

A Chump at Oxford

HAL ROACH—UNITED ARTISTS, 1940. *Six reels. Directed by Alfred Goulding. Scenario by Charles Rogers, Harry Langdon, and Felix Adler. Camera: Art Lloyd.*

With Laurel & Hardy, Forrester Harvey, James Finlayson, Wilfrid Lucas, Forbes Murray, Frank Baker, Eddie Borden, Gerald Rogers, Peter Cushing, Victor Kendall, Gerald Fielding, Charles Hall.

Street-cleaners Laurel & Hardy are instrumental in foiling a bank hold-up, and in gratitude the president of the bank asks them what reward he can bestow. They ask for, and receive, an education at England's Oxford University. While there, they suffer the customary hazing, including being given the Dean's quarters as their own, and get lost in the maze. Laurel is accidentally hit on the head, and a freak mental condition changes him into the reincarnation of a long-lost Oxford "great"—Lord Paddington, a thoroughly British mental wizard and sports champion. In this state he puts the other students to shame. and makes Hardy his personal lackey, before Hardy finally rebels, and a falling window sash hits him on the head again, restoring him to his former self.

It was potentially good news to have the Laurel & Hardy-Hal Roach combination together again, but conditions now were rather different. The comedy field of the 40's, exemplified by the pungent wit of Preston Sturges and the romantic farces of Cary Grant, were veering more and more away from sight comedy. With his studio going full blast on fairly elaborate features, the Laurel & Hardys were now Roach's *least* important product rather than the mainstay of his organization. In fact, the initial intention was to make them as featurettes, but because they still had more value as second features, a compromise was reached and they were made as short five-reelers. *A Chump at Oxford* was a welcome step up from from *The Flying Deuces,* but it was still a hastily assembled bag of old tricks, and far below their old standards. Once more Laurel masqueraded as a maid, and once more that old collegiate gag of planting the newcomers in the Dean's bedroom was played for all it was worth. One sequence in a maze, with a make-believe ghost, had genuine merit, although again its basic gag—a hand thrust through some shrubbery to give Laurel & Hardy a "third" hand—was an old one, having been done before by Charlie Chase and by Chaplin. The most original sequences in the film con-

As street-cleaners, outside the *Finlayson* National Bank! Finlayson's role in this film was brief, limited to an episode at the beginning where Ollie is a butler, and Stan repeats his female impersonation routine as a maid.

cerned Laurel's assuming the personality of the English nobleman; his condescending putting of "Fatty" in his place, and his indignation at a "debagging" ceremony, all done with a most convincing upper-crust British accent, represented some of Laurel's funniest screen scenes. They also enabled him to wiggle his ears, another of Laurel's physical accomplishments that were trotted out from time to time over the years.

A Chump at Oxford had many good scenes, but the film as a whole was loosely organized, with many dead spots. Its director, Alfred Goulding, was always a singularly uninspired film-maker whose comedies always had a tendency to fall flat. It is surely no coincidence that Laurel & Hardy had always avoided him when they had sole control over their films, and one can only conjecture that with a top director at the helm—a James Horne or a William Seiter—*A Chump at Oxford* might well have been a sufficiently good comedy to re-establish the comedians permanently.

After a blow on the head, Stan assumes the identity of Lord Paddington, to the gratification of dean Wilfrid Lucas and the consternation of Ollie, now relegated to a lackey's position.

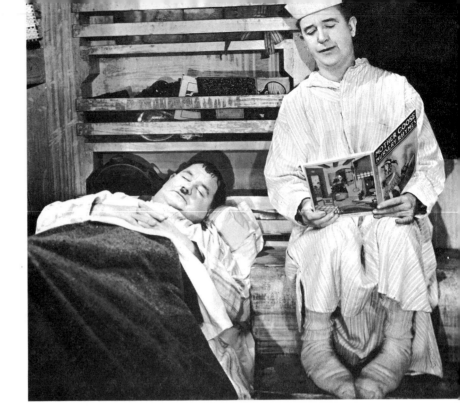

Saps at Sea

HAL ROACH–UNITED ARTISTS, 1940. *Five reels. Directed by Gordon Douglas. Scenario by Charles Rogers, Harry Langdon, Gil Pratt, and Felix Adler. Camera: Art Lloyd.*

With Laurel & Hardy, James Finlayson, Dick Cramer, Ben Turpin, Harry Bernard, Eddie Conrad.

Laurel & Hardy work in a horn factory, where the employees go beserk at fairly regular intervals. The constant honking of horns soon drives Hardy to a nervous breakdown, and Dr. Finlayson prescribes the peace and quiet of a sea voyage. Since Hardy cannot stand the ocean, they settle for renting a small and quite unseaworthy boat, in which they'll spend the convalescent period safely tied up in the harbor. But escaped killer Dick Cramer climbs aboard their craft at night and sets them adrift. Forced to serve him breakfast—and with no food to do it with—they concoct a nauseous meal from the materials at hand,

With Ben Turpin, a co-worker in the horn factory.

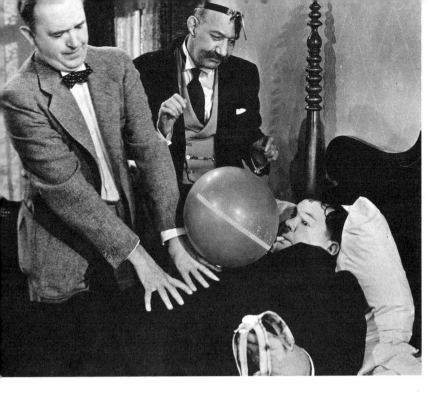

After his nervous breakdown, Ollie is tended by Dr. Finlayson.

lamp-wicks for bacon, string for spaghetti, and so forth. But the killer overhears their plans, and forces them to eat it before he kills them. Hardy, realizing that the sound of horns will turn him into a raging, fighting fool, tells Laurel to blow his trombone. He does, and the strategy works. But the trombone falls apart after Hardy has gotten in one telling blow, and now he is at the mercy of the enraged killer. While the slaughter goes on, Laurel struggles manfully to get the trombone together again, and manages to blow a few blasts just in time for Hardy to turn the tables. The harbor police come to arrest Cramer, and Hardy is a hero—until Laurel shows them how it was done, and after beating up the police force, Hardy finds himself heading for the same cell as the killer!

Saps at Sea had even less "plot" than its predecessor, and in structure seemed merely like two two-reelers strung together. The first half of the film was lively, fast-paced, violent and often quite brilliant slapstick. The horn factory sequence, though clearly borrowed from Chaplin's *Modern Times,* was very funny and led into equally good, and equally destructive, footage with James Finlayson, whose drastic methods included filling an outsize balloon with air from Hardy's lungs. But the second half of the film, taking place on the cramped boat set, floating in a studio tank, had the air of one of their weakest early sound shorts. The slapstick here became crude and forced, the gags drawn out far too long, and the meal sequence both unfunny and distasteful. Despite the vigor of the first half, *Saps at Sea* spiralled downhill very quickly, and was their first feature since *Pack Up Your Troubles* that really looked like a "B" picture. It was to be their last film for Hal Roach.

The synthetic meal: "*You* eat it!" growls Dick Cramer.

195

Veteran comedy director Malcolm St. Clair, who made most of the new Laurel & Hardy films for Fox.

1941

During the years 1941-45 Laurel & Hardy made eight more films, six for 20th Century-Fox and two for M-G-M. One final film was made in 1952. For the most part, these were poor and steadily worsening features, and Laurel & Hardy admirers were generally of the opinion that they should never have been made. Laurel himself, in later years, admitted that the films were weak, and blamed their poor quality on the fact that he and Hardy had no control over their shooting and were handed scripts with which they could not tamper. Undoubtedly they did miss the freedom they had enjoyed in their old Roach days. Fox was a big studio, costs of production in the 40's were mounting rapidly, and to leave a small and relatively unimportant unit alone to experiment and possibly disregard production schedules would have been considered a luxury.

In fairness to Fox, there doesn't seem to have been quite the deliberate design to sabotage Laurel & Hardy as has often been implied. Care seems to have

been taken to give them comedy directors best suited to their style. Malcolm St. Clair, a former master of silent comedy, an expert at both slapstick and sophisticated satire, directed the majority of their Fox films. As to scripts, they were so full—perhaps too full—of old and well-known Laurel & Hardy routines that it is absurd to suggest that Laurel & Hardy were never consulted on content. Perhaps the painful truth, and the truth that has always been avoided, is merely that the boys were tired and played out. They needed to take stock of themselves and experiment with fresh material—and this was something that there was no time for when they were committed to turn out six features. To add to the dilemma, Universal's new comedy team of Abbott & Costello had caught on like wildfire. Their films were slick, streamlined, full of action and songs, and very much attuned to wartime entertainment tastes. The Abbott & Costello films dated very quickly and seem quite tiresome today—even their best routines lacked the staying power of

196

Their new films abounded in reworkings of old routines, such as the sleeping-berth sequence from *Berth Marks,* which was re-used in *The Big Noise*.

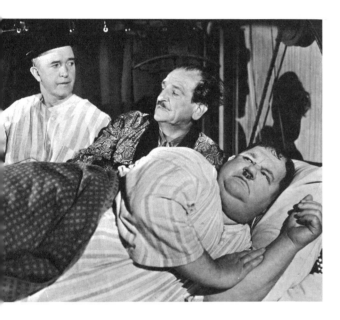

Laurel & Hardy's—but in the 40's they delivered what the public wanted, and they also captured the juvenile market which didn't remember the vintage Laurel & Hardy classics and understandably wasn't too impressed by their current output.

Inevitably too, Laurel and Hardy were growing old—and age can be a terrible thing for a comedian like Stan Laurel, whose forte is the projection of innocence. The added years hardly affected Oliver Hardy, whose screen image could logically mellow and mature with him. Age has never affected the comedy style of players like Charlie Ruggles or W. C. Fields, or even Maurice Chevalier, whose image was built on the sly, all-knowing *lack* of innocence. But

there were certain clowns to whom youth was essential—Stan Laurel, Harry Langdon, Buster Keaton. Once lines began to crease those bland baby-like faces and weight was added to their bodies, they were no longer the believable innocents, but instead old men retreating into infantilism. With brilliant material, they could still pull it off; but with average or mediocre material, which unfortunately proved to be their lot in later years, the act became tasteless and embarrassingly dull. Nothing Laurel & Hardy ever did in these later years was without interest; sometimes the old spark roared into flame again and we had brief gems of first-rate humor, but for the most part the decline was a painful one to watch.

Great Guns

20TH CENTURY FOX, 1941. *Seven reels. Produced by Sol M. Wurtzel. Directed by Monty Banks. Scenario by Lou Breslow. Camera by Glen Mac-Williams.*

With Laurel & Hardy, Sheila Ryan, Dick Nelson, Edmund MacDonald, Charles Trowbridge, Ludwig Stossel, Kane Richmond, Mae Marsh, Ethel Griffies, Paul Harvey.

Laurel & Hardy are retainers to a pampered son of a millionaire. The playboy is delighted when he is drafted, glad at last to be able to prove himself a man entirely on his own. But afraid that he is sickly and in need of protection, the boys get themselves drafted too, so they can be with him. However, he soon shows that he can stand on his own feet, while Laurel & Hardy are stuck with the inevitable tough sergeant.

The condescending stare and the pudgy forefinger were still key items in Hardy's repertoire—but *Great Guns* gave him too few moments like this in which to use them.

198

Some eighteen months after the release of *Saps at Sea,* Fox proudly announced the "return" of Laurel & Hardy in a big new series. To their credit, they spent money advertising the film, and got good bookings for it. (In England, where a wartime audience provided a ready market for comedy, it did exceptionally well). However, it's a pity that more of that enthusiasm and budget wasn't allocated to the film itself. Although it received surprisingly good reviews, it was a slow and ponderous effort, with far too much of the boy-girl plot, and too few good comedy sequences. In fact, the gags that stand out as highlights were the kind of gags that in earlier years would have been merely throwaways: a bridge constructing sequence resurrects that reliable gag of Laurel marching on screen holding a huge plank which is carried across the screen at some length to reveal Laurel on the *other* end as well; a shaving routine with a faulty lamp bulb; and some very mechanical stuff with a pet crow concealed in Hardy's trousers during inspection. The staleness of much of the material was emphasized by the fact that Abbott & Costello's first starring vehicle, *Buck Privates,* also an Army comedy with a tough sergeant and a playboy making good, had gone into release some six months earlier.

A-Haunting We Will Go

20TH CENTURY-FOX, 1942. *Six reels. Produced by Sol M. Wurtzel. Directed by Alfred Werker. Scenario by Lou Breslow. Camera: Glen Mac-Williams.*

With Laurel & Hardy, Dante the Magician, John Shelton, Sheila Ryan, Elisha Cook, Jr., Don Costello.

With the police hot on his trail, a gang leader hides in a coffin, hoping to outwit the police and claim an inheritance when the coffin reaches its destination. Laurel & Hardy are duped into escorting the coffin, but en route it is accidentally switched with that used by Dante the Magician in his magic act. The crooks go after Laurel & Hardy, who manage to turn the tables and hand them over to the law.

Their second comedy for Fox was an improvement over the first, thanks in some measure to Dante the Magician, a genial ham who worked well with them. But it was still a slowly paced film, and the comedians' lack of enthusiasm for their material was rather evident. Critics commented that their material seemed very dated. Nevertheless, despite a short runnnig time of only 67 minutes, the film secured top-of-the-bill bookings.

With Edgar Kennedy in some rather labored slapstick.

Air Raid Wardens

M-G-M, 1943. *Seven reels. Produced by B. F. Zeidman. Directed by Edward Sedgwick. Scenario by Martin Rackin, Jack Jevne, Charles Rogers, Harry Crane. Camera: Walter Lundin.*

With Laurel & Hardy, Edgar Kennedy, Jacqueline White, Horace (Stephen) McNally, Nella Walker, Donald Meek, Henry O'Neill, Howard Freeman, Paul Stanton, Robert Emmet O'Connor, William Tannen, Russell Hicks, Phil Van Zandt, Frederick Worlock, Don Costello.

Laurel & Hardy are air raid wardens who foil a Nazi plot to sabotage a magnesium plant.

Back at their old studio for the first time since *Blockheads,* with a good comedy director at the helm and with at least two of their former writers involved in the script, *Air Raid Wardens* was at least superficially better than their first two Fox films. It was slick and pleasantly amusing, but beyond that it offered little cause for enthusiasm. Reputedly, Civil Defense representatives, on hand as "advisors" managed to sidetrack any gags which seemed to cast aspersions on the efficiency of their organization! Reviewers commented that it "has child appeal only," was filled with "constant repetition" with "laughs few and labored," and that the "feature footage forces the boys to repeat themselves to the point of dullness."

Vivian Blaine helped to make *Jitterbugs* the best of their post-Roach films.

Jitterbugs

20TH CENTURY-FOX, 1943. *Eight reels. Produced by Sol M. Wurtzel. Directed by Malcolm St. Clair. Screeplay by Scott Darling. Camera: Lucien Andriot.*
With Laurel & Hardy, Vivian Blaine, Bob Bailey, Douglas Fowley, Noel Madison, Lee Patrick, Robert Emmett Keane, Charles Halton.

Laurel & Hardy cross swords with a gang of confidence men, and champion the cause of a night-club singer whose career the villains are trying to wreck.

Although almost plotless, by a happy combination of circumstances *Jitterbugs* emerged like an oasis in the desert of their current mediocrity, and was easily the

Crooks Noel Madison (left) and Douglas Fowley (right) try a little intimidation.

Oliver, posing as a Kentuckian of the old school, uses all of his charms on that "flower of Southern womanhood," Lee Patrick.

best of their final nine films. Wurtzel gave them a top director in Mal St. Clair, and he rose to the occasion on this film, although he too was tired, ill, and near the end of his career. (He remained the director on their three other Fox productions, though with less success.) And undoubtedly a major reason for the film's added merit was that Fox used it as an introductory showcase for their new singing star and potential Betty Grable replacement, Vivian Blaine. This involved allocating more money to production values, sets, and camerawork. A top cameraman was assigned (Lucien Andriot), and a first-class art direc-

tor (James Basevi). The results were handsome and showmanlike, while Vivian Blaine, a discovery of real note, added good songs and genuine personality to the proceedings. The better-than-usual comedy sequences allowed Laurel to masquerade as a fussy spinster, and Hardy as both a sheriff and a Southern colonel of the old school, whose gallant and chivalrous dialogue encounters with Lee Patrick were welcome throwbacks to such parallel sequences in *Way Out West* and earlier films. A good runaway showboat sequence provided a rousing slapstick finale.

The Dancing Masters

20TH CENTURY-FOX, 1943. *Six reels. Produced by Lee Marcus. Directed by Malcolm St. Clair. Scenario by Scott Darling and George Bricker. Camera: Norbert Brodine.*

With Laurel & Hardy, Trudy Marshal, Bob Bailey, Matt Briggs, Margaret Dumont, Allan Lane, Robert Mitchum, Nestor Paiva, George Lloyd, Edward Earle, Charles Rogers, Sperry Hall, Sam Ash, Bill Haade, Arthur Space, Daphne Pollard.

Laurel & Hardy operate a dancing school, Laurel teaching ballet and Hardy jive. The hero, Bob Bailey,

Robert Mitchum, a young player on the way up, sandwiched this small role in between villains in Hopalong Cassidy westerns.

203

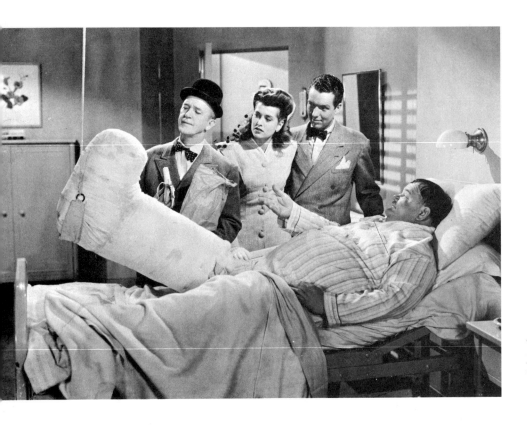

is a young inventor in love with a girl whose father, a millionaire, opposes their marriage. To help him promote his invention, Hardy tries to make money by a number of means, including taking out an accident insurance policy on Laurel with a group of insurance racketeers who benefit by killing off their policy holders. With Laurel & Hardy involved, the racketeers are captured, the invention proven, and the hero wins his sweetheart.

Although below the standards set by *Jitterbugs, The Dancing Masters* remained an amusing comedy, fast-paced despite its excess of plot, and with a good runaway bus sequence. Revived material included repetition of a sequence from *Thicker Than Water.* Laurel, however, was now getting rather too old to continue to be amusing in his dame masquerade, especially when clad in ballet skirt and tights.

The Big Noise

20TH CENTURY-FOX, 1944. *Seven reels. Produced by Sol M. Wurtzel. Directed by Malcolm St. Clair. Scenario by Scott Darling. Camera: Joe MacDonald.*

With Laurel & Hardy, Doris Merrick, Arthur Space, Veda Ann Borg, Bobby Blake, Frank Fenton, *Jack Norton, James Bush, Phil Van Zandt, Esther Howard, Robert Dudley, Edgar Dearing, Selmar Jackson, Harry Hayden, Francis Ford, Charles Wilson, Ken Christy, Beal Wong, Louis Arco.*

Laurel & Hardy are janitors for a private detective

Convincing Arthur Space that they are crack detectives.

Slapstick sequences such as this were pale and tedious shadows of the work they had done in their best Roach days.

agency who pass themselves off as sleuths and hire out to escort the inventor of a new super-bomb. Enemy agents are on the trail of the bomb, but Laurel & Hardy not only outwit them, but use the bomb to sink a Japanese submarine.

The Big Noise sank to a new low even for the post-Hal Roach features and was probably the worst of *all* the full-length Laurel & Hardy films. Highlights—such as a sequence in a "push-button" house, and an upper-berth sequence, re-worked from *Berth Marks* and also involving comic drunk Jack Norton—were few and far between. Reviewers termed it, "Poor—strictly for youngsters" and "No more than a whisper in the realm of comedy." And at 74 minutes, its padding really showed.

With Mary Boland and Henry O'Neill.

Nothing But Trouble

M-G-M, 1944. *Seven reels. Produced by B. F. Zeidman. Directed by Sam Taylor. Scenario by Russell Rouse and Ray Golden. Camera: Charles Salerno, Jr.*
With Laurel & Hardy, Mary Boland, Philip Merivale, Henry O'Neill, David Leland, John Warburton, Mathew Boulton, Connie Gilchrist.

Laurel & Hardy, chef and butler at a fashionable society mansion foil a plot by enemy agents to assassinate an exiled boy-king.

By virtue of its M-G-M mountings slightly better than

The Big Noise, Nothing But Trouble, despite a good comedy veteran in director Sam Taylor, was another weak entry in Laurel & Hardy's tragically fading career. There was far too much sentimental and ingenuous material devoted to the boy-king's wonderment at American democracy, and his desire to be "one of the fellows" and play football. Laurel & Hardy made the most of sequences in which they unintentionally wreck a dinner party, try to deprive a hungry lion of his steak, and teeter on skyscraper ledges, but even these episodes were loosely constructed and lacked genuine comic punch.

Laurel's age was really beginning to show by now.

207

The Bullfighters

20TH CENTURY-FOX, 1945. *Seven reels. Produced by William Girard. Directed by Malcolm St. Clair. Scenario by Scott Darling. Camera: Norbert Brodine.*

With Laurel & Hardy, Margo Woode, Richard Lane, Carol Andrews, Diosa Costello, Frank McGown, Ralph Sanford, Irving Gump, Ed Gargan, Lorraine De Wood, Emmett Vogan, Roger Neury, Gus Glassmire, Rafael Storm, Jay Novello, Robert Filmer, Hank Wordern, Guy Zanette, Jose Portugal, Max Wagner.

Laurel & Hardy are private detectives, who arrive in Mexico on the trail of a lady criminal. Coincidentally, Laurel is an exact double for a matador who appears to have vanished, and the anxious fight manager persuades Laurel to take his place in the bullring. But at the last minute the real matador arrives, and thus there are two Laurels on hand to confuse the bullring afficionados and the criminal.

Laurel & Hardy's last American film was a shapeless fiasco, perhaps not their very worst film, but not too far from it. Production values were a little above average, but there were few good gags and it was a sorry farewell to the screen for two of its greatest comedians.

Supporting players like Ralph Sanford didn't provide the kind of comic foils that the boys needed, and had had, in earlier years, in the shape of Walter Long, James Finlayson and Charlie Hall.

Atoll K

FORTEZZA FILMS *and* LES FILMS SIRIUS,
France, 1952. Nine reels. Also released as ROBINSON
CRUSOELAND *and* UTOPIA. *Produced by R. Elger.
Directed by John Berry and Leo Joannon.*

*With Laurel & Hardy, Suzy Delair, Max Elloy,
Adriano Rimoldi.*

Laurel & Hardy inherit a yacht and an island and set
out to sea accompanied by a stateless refugee who
offers to act as their cook in return for a home on
their island, and a stowaway. Their yacht founders in
a tropical storm, but providentially a newly created
atoll emerges from beneath the sea to save them.
Settling down in their new home, they are soon joined
by a girl fleeing from her jealous fiancée. Together
they organize the island as their own private Republic, and all goes well until uranium is discovered.
The nations of the world battle over ownership of
the atoll, and money-hungry adventurers swarm
there. The little party is about to be lynched when
another timely eruption sinks their atoll beneath the
waves once more. A passing ship rescues them. Suzy
is reunited with her now contrite fiancée, but Laurel
& Hardy, finally reaching their own island, find that
inheritance and other taxes are so staggering that
they must forget their dreams of a life of ease.

Laurel & Hardy's final film was almost as much of a
misfire as Chaplin's *A King in New York,* but it was

nevertheless a courageous effort to do something different, and in this respect at least it was a far more worthwhile venture than most of their later U.S. releases. But it was one of those unfortunate productions foredoomed to failure by budget limitations and problems of communication between a multi-lingual crew. Much of its political satire needed wit rather than visual humor or, better still, a delicate blending of both in the Preston Sturges manner. John Berry, a good director of taut melodramas, was clearly a totally unsuitable choice as the film's co-director, and commercially a suicidal one for any film with a political tinge (even a comic one), since he was then under a cloud in the United States as one of the "unfriendly" Communists. The film received but scant U.S. distribution in 1955, three years after its production, and no major distributor would touch it because of its difficult marketability and the problem of Berry's association with it. When it was finally released, it was cut by more than two reels, and curiously some of the funniest sight-gag sequences were among those deleted. Further hurting the film was the rather crude dubbing for the non-Laurel & Hardy roles, and most especially the appalling physical appearance of Stan Laurel himself. He had been extremely ill prior to and during production, and looked far older and sicker in this film than he did more than ten years later, just before his death. The shock of his appearance was such that his admirers didn't feel like laughing at him, and by the time this initial impact had worn off, it was too late to really warm up to the film. Nevertheless, it had a certain charm and was quite undeserving of the total obscurity into which it was hurled. Lacking in much of

Hardy with John Wayne in *The Fighting Kentuckian.*

210

the standard Laurel & Hardy humor (wisely, for they looked too old for their familiar knockabouts to be appealing or even to have any point), it substituted elements of whimsy and satire, and had much of the spirit of one of Douglas Fairbanks' last films, the breezy *Mr. Robinson Crusoe*. There was an abundance of sight gags, but most of them were bizarre gags for immediate reaction, more reminiscent of Buster Keaton than the carefully built routines of Laurel & Hardy. Typical gags: Laurel leaning out of the porthole during the hurricane to literally "pour oil on the troubled waters" (the mountainous waves instantaneously subside!); Laurel burping his pet lobster; and a wild episode in which a bat invades their cabin at night. Laurel chases it, gradually maneuvering it to the window. But when he opens the window, instead of the one bat flying *out,* a whole swarm of his comrades fly *in!* The dialogue, too, was often quite pointed and amusing, as in a good episode where Hardy allots the prime political posts of his new Republic, giving key positions to himself, Suzy Delair (a vivacious French actress, strangely lustreless here), and his other two cohorts. All of the governmental posts have been filled before Hardy gets to Stan, who is heartbroken that he has been ignored. But Hardy pacifies him with a magnificently diplomatic line: "Why Stanley, you're *The People!*"

Despite their age and the uncertainty of their surroundings, Laurel & Hardy keep the film going at a good clip. It falters only in the lengthy and tedious cutaway sequence to establish the boy-girl subplot, and in the climactic episodes when the commentary on political wrangling and the tyranny of mob rule is inevitably too heavy for the comedy balance to be maintained. However, the film brightens up again for its finale with an unexpected "black" joke. The stateless refugee, once more back to his old trade of trying to smuggle himself aboard outgoing ships, hides this time in a lion's cage. All that is left as the cage is swung aboard ship are his boots!

Atoll K was the last film in which Laurel & Hardy appeared together. Stan had made no appearance at all without Hardy since their initial teaming. Hardy worked in only three films without Stan: Hal Roach's *Zenobia* (1939); a serio-comic role in a 1949 John Wayne western, *The Fighting Kentuckian;* and a character comedy vignette in Frank Capra's *Riding High* in 1950.

The Compilations:

THE GOLDEN AGE OF COMEDY
(Robert Youngson Productions for DCA release, 1958)

WHEN COMEDY WAS KING
(Robert Youngson Productions for 20th Century-Fox, 1960)

DAYS OF THRILLS AND LAUGHTER
(Robert Youngson Productions for 20th Century-Fox, 1961)

THIRTY YEARS OF FUN
(Robert Youngson Productions for 20th Century-Fox, 1962)

212

M-G-M's Big Parade of Laughs.

M-G-M'S BIG PARADE OF LAUGHS
(Robert Youngson Productions for M-G-M, 1964)

LAUREL & HARDY'S LAUGHING TWENTIES
(Robert Youngson Productions for M-G-M, 1965)

THE CRAZY WORLD OF LAUREL & HARDY
(Jay Ward Productions, 1966)

THE FURTHER PERILS OF LAUREL & HARDY
(Robert Youngson Productions, 1967)

Laurel & Hardy's features and shorts have never stopped playing, although often in abominably mutilated and confusingly retitled versions, both in theatres and on TV, but it is to *The Golden Age of Comedy* that most of the credit must go for a renaissance of real interest in the work of Laurel & Hardy, both from the public and from the critics. A compilation of great sight gag material from the 20's, primarily from the Roach and Sennett stables, it devoted approximately half of its running time to generous samplings of outstanding silent Laurel & Hardy comedies. Footage that was fresh because it had lain unseen for so long astonished laughter-convulsed audiences with the scope and variety of their comedy — and sur-

The Golden Age of Comedy.

Laurel & Hardy's Laughing Twenties.

prised them with the flawless pictorial quality achieved by printing from the original negatives. From this rebirth of interest in Laurel & Hardy, a number of things developed: Art-house acceptance of Laurel & Hardy, festivals of their films; and retrospective series at archives and museums throughout the world. Hardy lived just long enough to see the beginnings of this renaissance and to be gratified by it; Laurel lived long enough to be a part of it and to be voted an honorary Academy Award. After his death, television offered a banal and insulting "tribute" to the two comedians, and their old films, given yet another lease on life on TV, were supplemented by a series of cartoons which, contrary to expectation, often managed surprisingly well to capture the spirit and comic style of Laurel & Hardy.

The Youngson compilations offered generous portions not only from their well-known silent classics, such as *Big Business* and *Two Tars,* but resurrected such forgotten classics as *The Battle of the Century* as well as films that were never classics but still had

much to delight the eye and mind (*Wrong Again*) and representative samplings of their solo work. One can quibble with some of Youngson's methods: the earlier films tended to be overburdened with unnecessary (albeit informative and seriously intended) narration, and too often carefully built and methodically developed comedy sequences were edited to the bone, rushing right to the crux of the jokes, as though Laurel & Hardy were all speed, violence, and fast slapstick. But a compilation is a film apart, with a responsibility to itself as well as to its source material; it must create its own pattern and rhythm, and too much time devoted to an individual ingredient means both a disruption of that rhythm, and a less generous totality of highlights. Laurel & Hardy purists may well dispute Youngson's handling of certain favorite and well-remembered sequences, but there can be no disputing the taste and love he has put into these compilations, the skill with which they have been edited, or the unbounded delight they have brought to audiences who have been introduced to Laurel & Hardy

The Crazy World of Laurel & Hardy.

The Further Perils of Laurel & Hardy.

for the first time through them. The merits of the Youngson films stand out in even starker relief when compared with a rather stolid and unimaginative effort from a different producer, called *The Crazy World of Laurel & Hardy*. Dealing only summarily with the silents and concentrating primarily on the talkies, it uses far too many excerpts for any of them to build properly (three times as many films are represented as in any of the Youngson films), presents films out of chronological sequence, abuses editorial license to the extent of re-arranging the order of shots as they appeared in original sequence, and fails to identify many of the items used. The genius of Laurel & Hardy survives even such cavalier treatment to make *The Crazy World of Laurel & Hardy* an enjoyable diversion — but it's good to know that it will not be the last such compilation, and that there will be further Youngson mining of the Laurel & Hardy vaults in the future.

Deleted Scenes

A roundup of some of the many intriguing and frustrating stills that exist of sequences shot for Laurel & Hardy films and deleted prior to release.

With Tiny Sanford in a rockpile episode from *The Second Hundred Years*.

An intriguing and bizarre masquerade with midgets, shot for, but deleted from, *Their Purple Moment*.

A curious moment from *Liberty*. Tom Kennedy is on the left, yet in the released version he is not involved in this sequence at all, and appears—briefly—only in the opening scene as a prison guard.

217

The warden's daughter apparently involved in some fire drill, while the hole beneath the net suggests a prior Hardy descent, yet there is no hint of any such sequence in the final version of *Pardon Us*.

Another cut episode from *Pardon Us*, with the boys apparently having reached a ripe old age.

A deleted piece of slapstick with blacksmith Lionel Belmore in *Bonnie Scotland*.

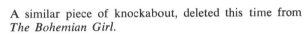

A similar piece of knockabout, deleted this time from
The Bohemian Girl.

Other than Chaplin, few comedians have been copied as much as Laurel & Hardy. Germany and Japan both had comedy teams that were out-and-out imitations, and even in the United States an inferior comedy team copied their costumes and gags in a cheap series of comedies in the late 20's. Cartoons, too, have constantly used gag caricatures of them, as for example this 1935 Disney cartoon, *Mickey's Polo Team*.

Hollywood's lack of concern for its *own* historical accuracy is shown by this tableau in the Hollywood Wax Museum. Not only is there no such scene in *A Perfect Day*, but there isn't even a "Bijou Theatre" as indicated by the clapper board. Nor does Edgar Kennedy (cast as a gout-ridden relative) appear as a cop!

223